150 Best Kitchen Ideas

150 Best Kitchen Ideas

COLLINS DESIGN
An Imprint of HarperCollins Publishers

HarperCollins books may be purchased for educational, business, or sales promotional use.
For information, please write: Special Markets Department, HarperCollins*Publishers*,
10 East 53rd Street, New York, NY 10022.

First published in 2008 by:
Collins Design
An Imprint of HarperCollins*Publishers*
10 East 53rd Street
New York, NY 10022
Tel.: (212) 207-7000
Fax: (212) 207-7654
collinsdesign@harpercollins.com
www.harpercollins.com

Distributed throughout the world by:
HarperCollins*Publishers*
10 East 53rd Street
New York, NY 10022
Fax: (212) 207-7654

Executive editor:
Paco Asensio

Editorial Coordinator:
Simone K. Schleifer

Assistant Editorial Coordinator:
Aitana Lleonart

Editor and texts:
Montse Borràs, Aitana Lleonart

Art director:
Mireia Casanovas Soley

Design and layout coordination:
Claudia Martínez Alonso

Layout:
Anabel Naranjo

Library of Congress Control Number: 2008944034

ISBN: 978-0-06-170440-6

Printed in China
First Printing, 2009

Contents

Introduction

The kitchen is one of the most important rooms in any home. Indeed, the hearth has existed since the first dwelling houses were erected and, in addition to serving as an area for cooking food, it was also used to heat the home. The amount of space available is a decisive factor when designing a kitchen, as this will determine the choice and layout of the different elements. If the kitchen is spacious, the different work areas can be clearly separated in order to make cooking more comfortable: a long worktop to prepare the food, a cooking area, a washing-up area and multiple combinations for the layout of electrical appliances and the storage of kitchenware and utensils. In small kitchens, on the other hand, the objective is to combine all of these functions into a small space and to find the most practical solution possible. Resistance and easy maintenance are the main factors to consider when choosing materials for a kitchen. While steel and wood are two of the most popular materials, marble and other more innovative materials, such as Silestone and Corian, are gradually appearing on the market. With the boom in loft type housing, a new type of kitchen has emerged. This no longer requires an enclosed space, but opens onto the other rooms in the house, especially the living and dining areas. This concept has since been introduced to other types of housing, including apartments and detached houses. In many kitchens of this kind islands are used to visually separate the kitchen from the other areas of the home. No matter what the type of kitchen—whether integrated, separate, large or small—there are no shortage of ideas or accessories to make cooking a much more comfortable and pleasant experience.

WOOD

Softbox Apartment

This project is the result of renovating an old apartment in Warsaw, which the owner inherited from his grandmother. Because there are windows on both sides of the apartment, it was decided to create an open-plan area containing all of the rooms, except the kitchen and bathroom, which were built into a block at one end of the apartment.

Architect: Centrala Designers
Task Force
Location: Warsaw, Poland
Date of construction: 2008
Photography: Nicolas Grospierre

1

The module, lined in wood,
contains the bathroom, while
the kitchen is at the side,
facing the rest of the
apartment.

Drawing

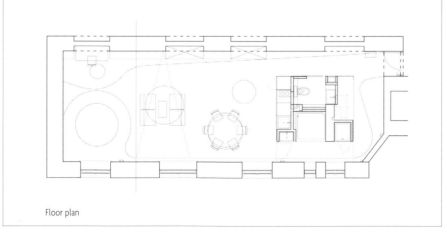

Floor plan

2

The different colored wood and the uneven layout of the panels at the front of the kitchen house several cupboards, behind which we have the larder, electrical appliances and storage space.

G+FM

This home was a garage prior to renovation. Every effort was made to preserve the original atmosphere, respecting both the volumes and materials: stone, concrete and wood. The kitchen work area visually breaks up the furniture and leaves the worktop and Corian panel in view.

Architect: Pensando en blanco
Location: Hondarribia, Guipúzcoa, Spain
Date of construction: 2007
Photography: Galder Izaguirre

The lighting is positioned in the lower part of the cupboards over the gap, and consists of fluorescent tubes with matt diffuser shades.

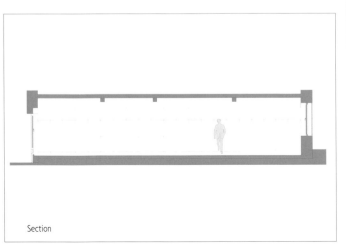

Section

3

In this case the kitchen has been built into the central unit of the house, a large oak closet with simple and straight lines. A reticular construction comprised of twenty-one 65 cm-wide modules.

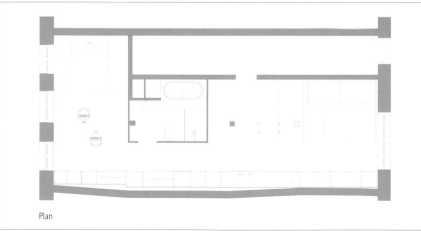

Plan

This kitchen is comprised of adaptable modules and designed for homes where the kitchen and lounge occupy a single space. This is from the Meg Collection, by Cesar, and is mainly comprised of fiberboard of wood with a melamine finish.

Meg Collection

Manufacturer: Cesar Cucine
Photography: Cesar Cucine

4

These versatile mid-height shelves can be combined with different modules to create a variety of effects. The shelves mark the transition point from the kitchen to the living room.

Kitchen A Surfside Residence

Architect: Stelle Architects
Location: Bridgehampton,
New York, USA
Date of construction: 2008
Photography: Stelle Architects

Because this kitchen is a vital space and sometimes workshop for the owners, it has to be both functional and aesthetic. As it forms part of the lounge area, a range of colours from the "sea foam" collection have been chosen for the décor.

Some of the kitchen utensils like pots, pans and colanders are hung over the island creating the impression of a restaurant kitchen; this not only looks good, but is also functional and saves storage space in cupboards and drawers.

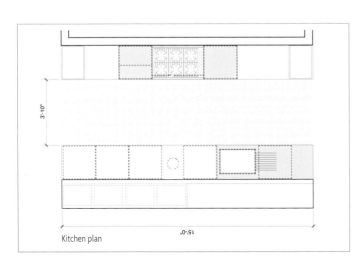

Kitchen plan

3'-10"

15'-0"

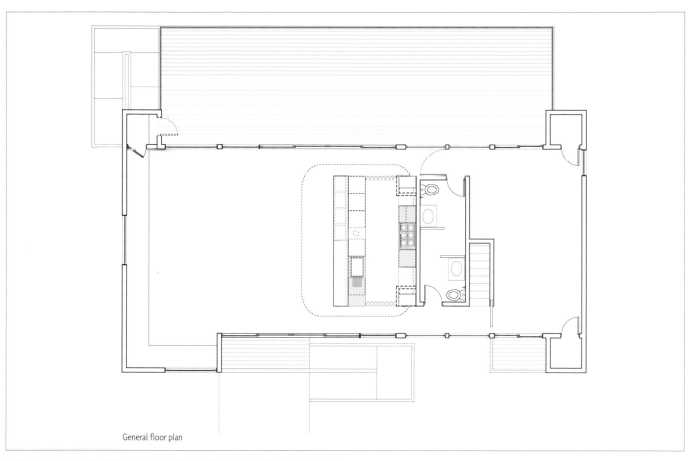

General floor plan

Materials such as stone, maple wood, stainless steel and latex, for the floor, have been chosen to indicate the different functions of each area or surface.

40 Mercer Kitchen

These kitchens are located in the 40 Mercer Street building in New York, the first project designed by the prestigious US architect Jean Nouvel. The kitchens come in a variety of models to suit the different house layouts: corner kitchens, wall kitchens and kitchens with central islands, among others.

Architect: Jean Nouvel
Manufacturer: Dada Contract
Location: New York, USA
Date of construction: 2007
Photography: Dada Contract

5

A combination of different shades and high quality woods, such as oak, wengé and dibetou, give it an elegant and sophisticated look.

This kitchen was built onto the back patio of the house. The flooring visually unites the two areas. A large central unit is used to hold the electrical appliances, cooking area, bookcase and storeroom, and extends to the lounge where it becomes a study unit.

Rozelle House

Architect: Tom Ferguson Architecture & Design
Location: Sydney, Australia
Date of construction: 2006
Photography: Simon Kenny

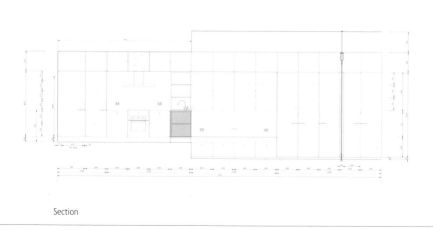

Section

6

The old façade, together with the window, has been preserved in its original state and is used as an interior wall to separate the lounge from the other rooms.

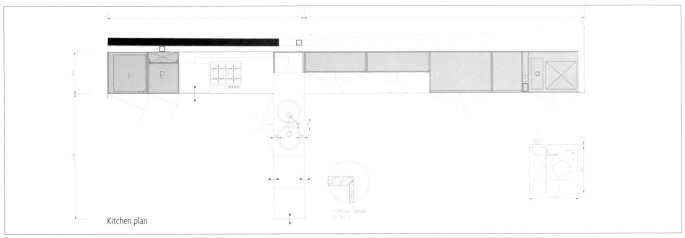

Kitchen plan

Located beside the living and dining rooms, this kitchen is the heart of the home. As is the case with the rest of the house, the materials used are natural and have a country look.

Downing Residence

Architect: Ibarra Rosano
Design Architects
Location: Tucson, Arizona, USA
Date of construction: 2004
Photography: Bill Timmerman

The island is made of local mesquite
wood and matches the custom-made
birch cupboards.

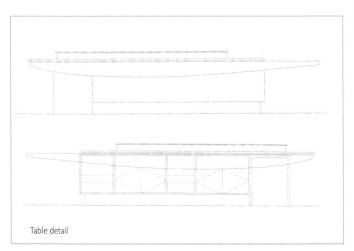

Table detail

The skylights at the entrance bathe the stone walls in natural light and enable the occupants to watch the light change with the different times of day and seasons of the year.

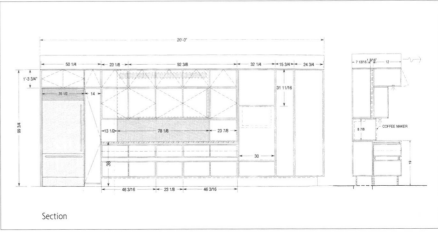

Section

Counter top detail

7

The unit with the cupboards not only serves as a larder and storage space, it also holds the house's heating and air-conditioning systems.

Two large skylights make this an open-air like kitchen. Different floor levels separate the working and eating areas. A wide variety of materials have been used, including terrazzo flooring, lacquered wall panels to reflect the light, and rosewood finishes.

St Paul's Place

Architect: **Project Orange**
Location: **London, UK**
Date of construction: **2006**
Photography: **Gareth Gardner**

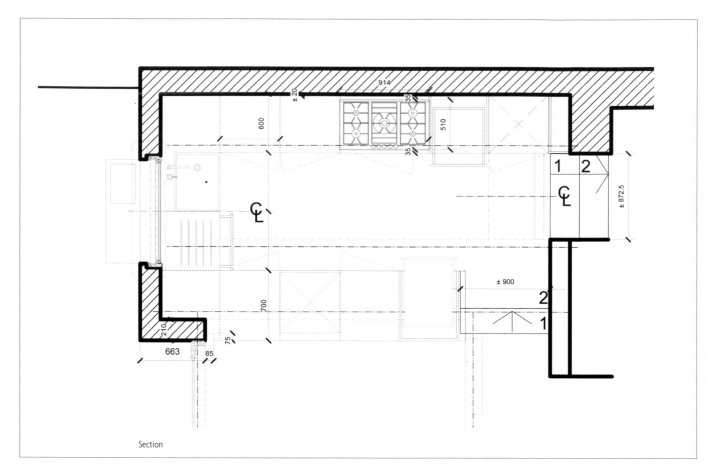

Section

914
± 20
600
35
510
35
1 2
C
L
± 872.5
C
L
± 900
2
1
700
210
75
663 85

8

A long light bulb runs along the length of the kitchen unit, lighting the flooring and bottom of the module to create a warm atmosphere.

Orange Cottage

This house is clearly influenced by the Tudor style of the village where it is located. Timeless materials, like brick, plaster and oak, have been chosen to create a contemporary yet functional look. The kitchen benefits from its proximity to the garden.

Architect: Project Orange
Location: Lavenham, Suffolk, UK
Date of construction: 2007
Photography: Jonathan Pile

9

All cupboard doors and panels are of 18 mm-MDF with a moisture-resistant, matt oak finish.

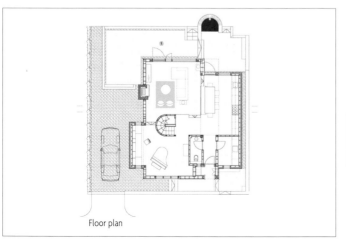

Floor plan

House in Brione

This house has privileged views of the town of Locarno and is surrounded by mountains and a lake. Continuous and level paving from the patio to the kitchen creates a link between the two areas.

Architect: Markus Wespi &
Jérôme de Meuron Architects
Location: Brione, Switzerland
Date of construction: 2005
Photography: Hannes Henz

10

This kitchen, which was custom designed and built, creates a synergy between the two main elements in the landscape outside, stone and wood.

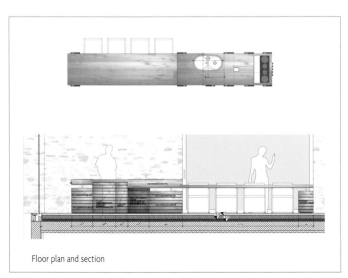

Floor plan and section

Small Kitchen House DB

This small 8 m² kitchen opens onto the lounge. The use of uniform furniture surfaces and a door opening onto the patio make it look more spacious than it actually is. The storage space was designed to make the most of the room available, without relinquishing the aesthetic.

Architect: Carolina Nisivoccia
Location: Milan, Italy
Date of construction: 2007
Photography: Paolo Utimpergher,
Paolo Riolzi

The materials used include green marble for the floor, oak for the doors of the kitchen units and steel for the back of the stove and island.

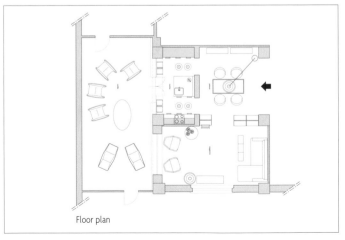

Floor plan

The U shaped layout of the cupboards in this kitchen facilitates contact with the exterior and lounge area, while optimising the work space. Recycled wood, and simple and practical finishes have been used in the carpentry.

Kitchen B Surfside Residence

Architect: **Stelle Architects**
Location: Bridgehampton,
New York, USA
Date of construction: 2008
Photography: **Stelle Architects**

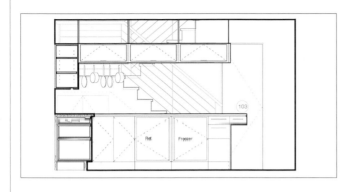

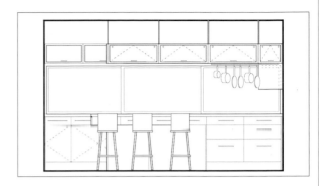

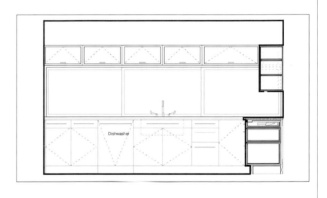

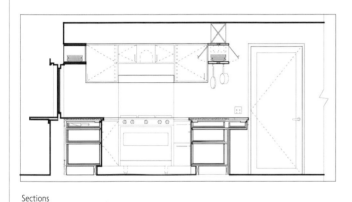

Sections

Kitchen floor plan

11

The wall units—with glass
doors—are lit from the inside
to showcase the kitchenware,
as well as to provide light to
the worktop below.

WOOD

Inspirations

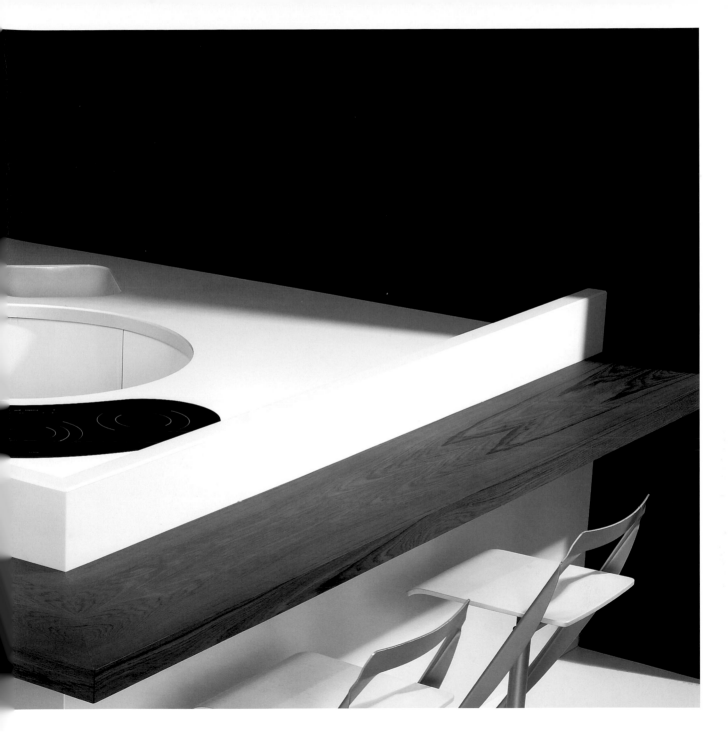

LACQUERED

Red and white are used to emphasize the volume of this kitchen and to energize the original concept of a versatile space on different levels. Technical details are highlighted in the furniture, lighting, wiring and smaller details.

Dejardin A. Residence

Architect: Pierre Hebbelinck
Location: Comblain-au-Pont, Belgium
Date of construction: 2004
Photography: Marie-Françoise Plissart

12

The auxiliary kitchen unit and a second set of stairs disappear behind the surface of the pull-out module which divides the room in two.

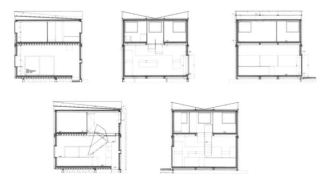

Sections

B1 collection

Manufacturer: **Bulthaup**
Photography: **Bulthaup**

Bulthaup presents an elegant line all in white with subtle details in brushed steel. The clean and flat surfaces are free of adornments. B1 consists of configurable modules with a choice of laminated, veneered, stainless steel, wood or glass finishes.

Drawing

13

Steel, glass, solid wood, plywood and colours like alpine white, gray and graphite highlight the purity of the whole.

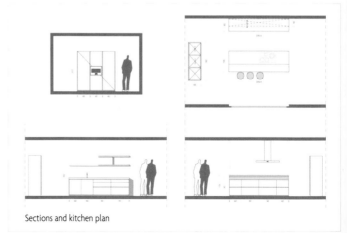

Sections and kitchen plan

The Cromatic modules can be used to hold electrical appliances. In the white model, some of the doors are of glass with a ground finish, and the black model, without doors, is very versatile for kitchens in living areas. The aluminum bar also serves as a handle.

Manufacturer: Ebanis
Photography: Ebanis

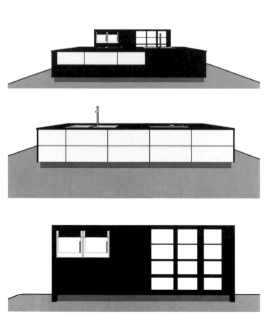

Diagram black kitchen

14

The kitchen island has pull-out modules with L-shaped fronts. Lacquered wengé is a highly resistant yet light material.

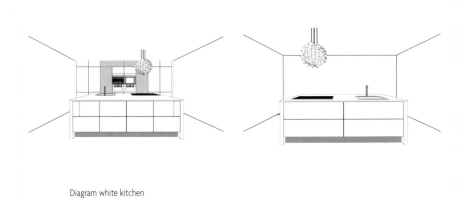

Diagram white kitchen

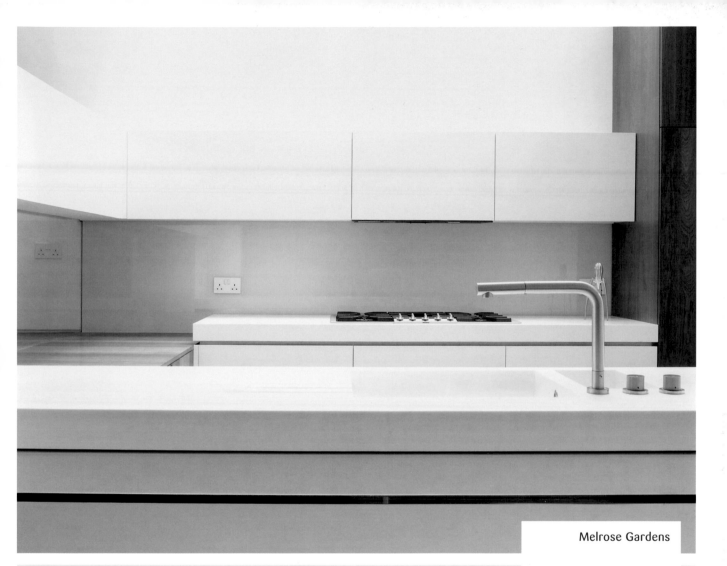

Melrose Gardens

Architect: SCAPE Architects
Location: London, UK
Date of construction: 2007
Photography: Michele Panzieri

This project is the result of an extension of a house in East London. The living room and kitchen have been combined into one, and although they are situated on two different levels, they share common elements and are separated only by a glass panel.

The kitchen is the focal point of the
home thanks to the powerful light from
the skylight in the ceiling.

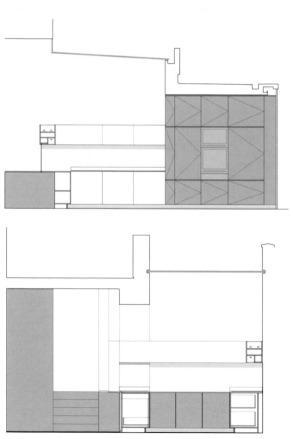

Sections

15

The wall units of the kitchen serve as a balustrade for the lounge area, the floor of which also doubles up as a worktop for the kitchen.

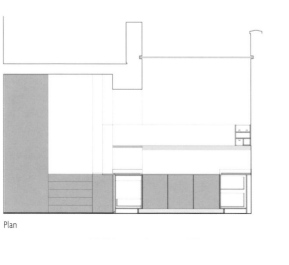

Plan

All of the communal areas in this home are combined into one open-plan space. Just a step separates the lounge area from the kitchen and dining room, where a stone wall and teakwood table give it a rustic look.

I+GA

Architect: Pensando en blanco
Location: Hondarribia, Guipúzcoa, Spain
Date of construction: 2007
Photography: Galder Izaguirre

16

The shelves and fridge are hidden behind a hinged ipe door beside the kitchen, which helps to maintain the warmth and harmony of the space.

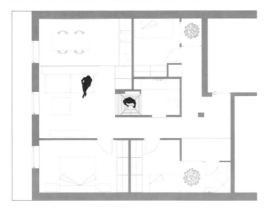

Floor plan

The Luce de Cesar collection features tempered lacquered glass for maximum resistance and is available in eleven different colours. The worktops also come with a glass finish, with thicknesses ranging from four or six centimeters.

Luce Collection

Manufacturer: **Cesar Cucine**
Photography: **Cesar Cucine**

17

The exterior aluminum handles can be replaced with practical interior opening devices to obtain a completely flat surface.

This house overlooks the Wien River Valley and the mountains and woods of Vienna. Communal areas like the dining room, kitchen and living room are combined into a single space.

House Hofman

Architect: Acn+ Architektur
Location: Vienna, Austria
Date of construction: 2006
Photography: Miran Kambič

18

This kitchen forms a module that divides the day and the night areas. The glass panel behind the worktop connects both spaces and distributes the light.

Floor plan

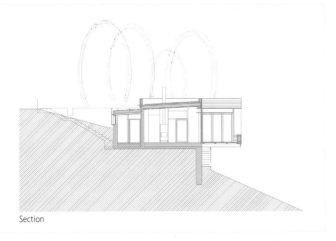

Section

19

A cylindrical burner has been installed at one end of the kitchen, which, in addition to being useful in this area, also heats the living area.

Fink House

Architect: Ian Moore Architects
Location: Sydney, Australia
Date of construction: 2005
Photography: Brett Boardman

The first floor of this newly renovated house, which was built in the mid 20th century, is divided into four, almost identical square-shaped areas that house the patio, garage, lounge and kitchen-dining room.

20

A passageway was left between the dining table and the cooking area to allow access to the lounge. All of the elements are long in order to make the most of the space available.

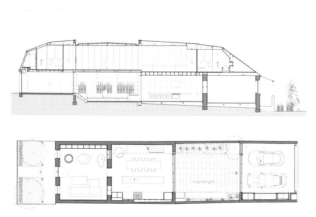

Section and floor plan

Home 02

White is the dominant color in this kitchen, and abundant natural light further enhances the feeling of purity. As is the case with the rest of the apartment, the purity of white contrasts with the country feel of the wood that lines the adjoining wall.

Architect: i29 Architects
Location: Amsterdam, The Netherlands
Date of construction: 2008
Photography: i29

21

One side of the kitchen opens
onto the rest of the house,
allowing the light to penetrate
to the interior and creating the
impression of more space.

Floor plan and section

Pool Kitchen

This kitchen was designed for interior and outdoor use. It features an enormous sliding glass door over the worktop. The materials were chosen on the basis of two criteria: a minimum of maintenance and a contemporary design.

Architect: Belzberg Architects
Location: Brentwood,
California, USA
Date of construction: 2007
Photography: Art Gray

22

In order to blend the interior with the exterior, the same materials and elements were used on both sides.

Kitchen plan

House in Hamburg

The premises on which the entire project was based were also taken into account when designing the kitchen: a minimalist design. The apartment was designed for rest and tranquility. The kitchen, therefore, has been restricted to the most basic functions.

Architect: Nieberg Architect
Location: Hamburg, Germany
Date of construction: 2006
Photography: Axel Nieberg

23

The storage area in front of the worktop is comprised of a floor-to-ceiling closet in matt white to match the walls.

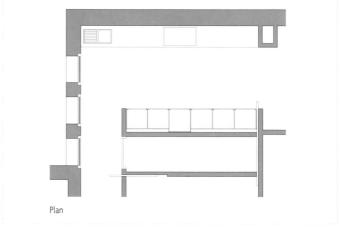

Plan

24

The oven is built into the closet and hidden by a vertically sliding door. When closed, it is completely invisible.

Section

The aim of this project was to achieve integration, continuity and functionality through a common element. In the end, the kitchen worktop-bar was positioned in such a way that it connects with the other spaces, i.e., the lounge and the dining room.

Apartment in Fornells

Architect: Argemí Falguera
Arquitectura
Location: Fornells, Menorca, Spain
Date of construction: 2007
Photography: Jaume Falguera

The central island can be
converted into a passageway
to connect all of the spaces or
used as a partition to separate
the areas.

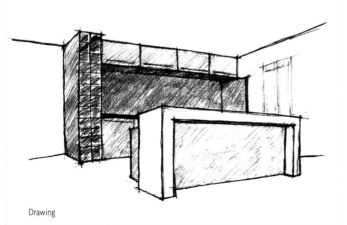

Drawing

Each color plays a decisive role. White, which is used extensively throughout the home, is the canvas, creating a sharp contrast with the black, and red lends the overall composition a note of color.

Floor plan

This project is a perfect example of how to clearly define kitchen, living and dining areas that are directly connected to one another. A panel open on both sides separates the two areas and a small window creates a visual link between the kitchen and the diners.

House in Aichtal

Architect: **Klumpp & Klumpp Architekten**
Location: **Aichtal, Germany**
Date of construction: **2005**
Photography: **Zooey Brown**

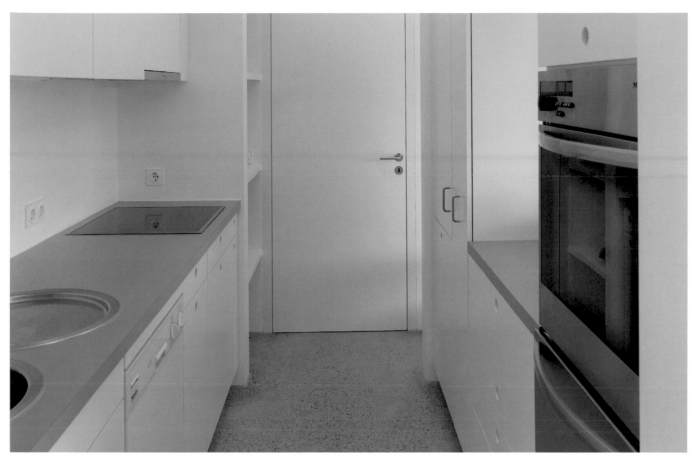

27

This small kitchen was designed to maximize its storage space capacity. It also benefits of abundant natural light thanks to generous openings.

Penthouse in Liege

Architect: Julie Brion & Tanguy
Leclercq
Location: Liege, Belgium
Date of construction: 2008
Photography: Laurent Brandajs

This penthouse is located in a modern building in the heart of Liège (Belgium). The kitchen, living room and dining room are all in the same area. An 8-meter panel was used to separate the day from the night areas.

Resistant materials have been used in the
kitchen, such as white laquered wood
and *Marrone Etrusco* stone in the
worktops and flooring.

Floor plan

28

The small wall that protrudes slightly from behind the kitchen island prevents the sink and worktop from being seen from the dining and living area.

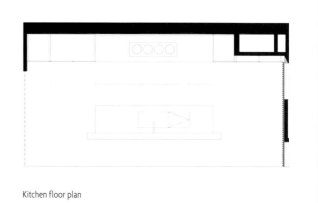

Kitchen floor plan

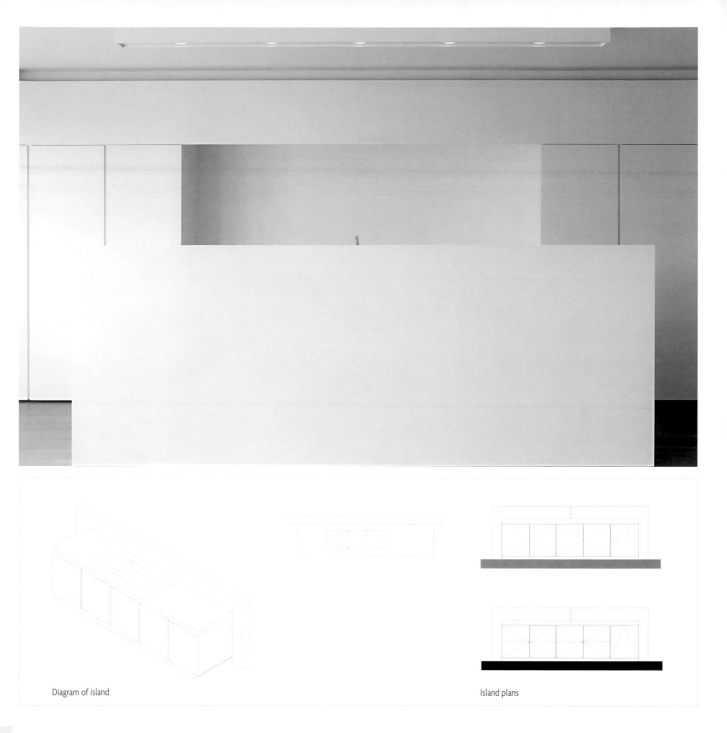

Diagram of island

Island plans

Ristretto collection

Manufacturer: Ebanis
Photography: Ebanis

This composition has two clearly differentiated sides: on the one hand, it is a typical kitchen for cooking and washing with storage modules for the electrical appliances; on the other, the lounge side with the wengé panel features a pull-out table and open modules on a shelf.

29

The perforated wooden boxes are part of the series and add to the versatility of a space that has to serve as both a kitchen and living area.

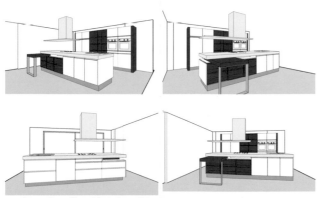

Diagram kitchen

Scavolini Baccarat

Manufacturer: **Scavollini**
Photography: **Scavollini**

Classical yet industrial, this kitchen stands out for its glossy lacquered finishes, large cupboards and granite worktops. The tall sliding drawers with sophisticated Plexiglass handles are a perfect marriage between functionality and aesthetics.

30

The cupboards with pull-out fronts come in heights ranging from 73 to 103 cm and can be placed on the floor, wall or kitchen islands.

Rendering

ZZ House

Architect: **Filippo Bombace**
Location: **Rome, Italy**
Date of construction: **2007**
Photography: **Luigi Filetici**

With the aim of achieving a more spacious look, this kitchen also serves as the dining area of this home. Minimalist lines and select materials were used to create a serene, elegant and bright area. A large oak panel connects the kitchen and the living area.

The sobriety of the lacquered furniture,
glass table and large windows is offset by
the warmth of the parquet floor.

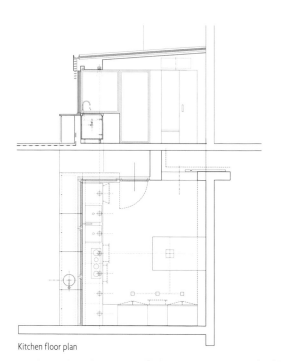

Kitchen floor plan

31

The electrical appliances and cupboards have been placed against the walls and hidden under smooth even surfaces in the dining area.

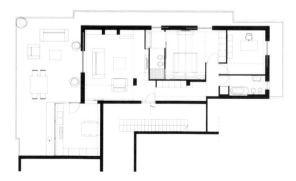

Floor plan

© Binova

LACQUERED

Inspirations

STEEL

Big Kitchen House DB

This spacious kitchen allows the owners, who are used to having good views, to cook with the maximum of comfort. A large window separates two very different zones: the hot area with the microwave and oven, and the cold area with two fridges and a freezer.

Architect: Carolina Nisivoccia
Location: Milan, Italy
Date of construction: 2007
Photography: Paolo Utimpergher, Paolo Riolzi

32

The working area, comprised
of a T-shaped island, has
several independent hobs
(induction cooktops, gas, etc.)
for different types of cooking.

Floor plan

On the other end of the kitchen, there is a comfortable table for working beside the larder with several spices and pictures of the best recipes.

This apartment has privileged views of the Coliseum in Rome. The kitchen stands out for its simplicity and glossy pearl gray and black finishes, which contrast with the yellow of the opposite wall. It also has a small breakfast ledge.

Apartment near the Coliseum

Architect: **Filippo Bombace**
Location: **Rome, Italy**
Date of construction: **2006**
Photography: **Luigi Filetici**

33

Because this kitchen is quite diminutive, the fridge and larder have been placed in the hallway leading to the living room and are hidden behind closets with no handles.

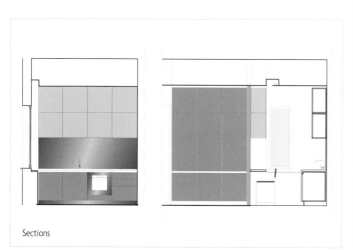

Sections

In this kitchen, the central units and rear wall are used as storage space in order to provide an uncluttered view. The structure descends from the back-lit suspended ceiling to support the storage wall and electrical appliances.

Beuth Residence

Architect: Beuth Residence
Location: Los Angeles, California, USA
Date of construction: 2005
Photography: John Linden

34

This limestone piece serves as a bench and low partition between the living and dining areas.

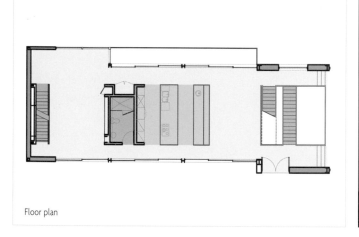

Floor plan

The country feel of wood and the sobriety of steel contrast in this project but also complement one another to create a warm and modern atmosphere. The electrical appliances and larder have been placed against the wall to keep the island free for working.

Duplex in Sarriá

Architect: Samsó & Associats
Location: Barcelona, Spain
Date of construction: 2005
Photography: Jordi Miralles

Manufacturer: **Alessi**
Photography: **Alessi**

Glass is a prominent feature of the different work areas and shelving of this kitchen, which has soft curved lines. The glass and wooden pieces are recyclable and have been covered in water paint to eliminate solvent emissions.

35

Curved shapes were chosen to create an atmosphere of warmth, nourishment and family ties.

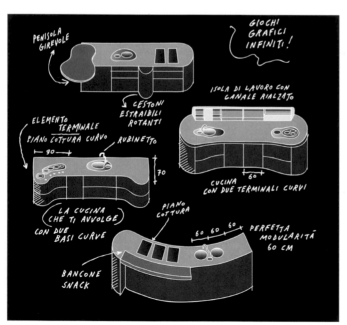

Drawings

The layout was determined by the cane vault, which was encased and limed in the traditional manner. In the center, an overhead skylight provides plenty of natural light and is equipped with solar panels.

House in L'Empordà

Architect: Lizarriturry Tuneu
Location: L'Empordà, Spain
Date of construction: 2006
Photography: José Luis Hausmann

The flooring throughout the house is of natural clay from the area, which was also used in the kitchen to maintain a harmonious look.

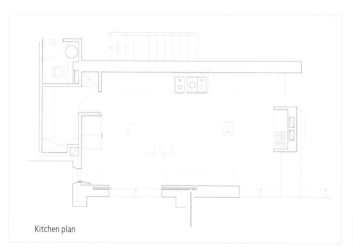

Kitchen plan

36

All of the furniture units were made to measure and have exclusive details like leather handles in the drawers.

The focal point of the kitchen is the central island of honed and polished stainless steel, which is where the food is prepared.

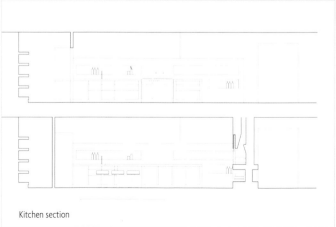

Kitchen section

Apartment in Barcelona

This apartment in Barcelona is a truly functional space with impeccable aesthetics, thanks to the hidden wall units, clear-cut lines and the use of steel. The lights under the wall units provide additional light to the working area.

Architect: Jordi Galí & Estudi
Location: Barcelona, Spain
Date of construction: 2000
Photography: Jordi Miralles

Ronçana House

This residence is located to the southeast of the Collserola mountain range in the town of Vallvidrera (Barcelona). The floor, floor-to-ceiling closets and dining table are made entirely of wood, which contrasts sharply with the steel in the working and cooking areas of the kitchen.

Interior Designer: **Adela Cabré**
Location: **Vallvidrera, Barcelona, Spain**
Date of construction: 2005
Photography: **Jordi Miralles**

© Fagor

STEEL

Inspirations

© Ernesto Meda

© Ernesto Meda

STONE

This kitchen has an L-shaped layout in which the different elements are distributed. In one area, we have the cooking zone with a long worktop and the sinks in front. In the other, a large furniture unit holds the electrical appliances and more storage space.

Weedan House

Architect: Stephen Jolson
Architects
Location: Toorak, Victoria,
Australia
Date of construction: 2006
Photography: Shania Shegedyn

37

The different materials clearly differentiate the function of each area. The cooking area is of steel, the working area has a marble worktop, and the rest of the furniture is lacquered.

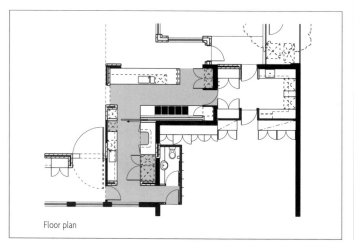

Floor plan

Grand Relais Kitchen

Grand Relais is a kitchen with a neo-classical spirit, as apparent from the finishes and details, like the 15 cm fixed or pull-out doors with baskets. The logo knobs provide the finishing touch to a push-pull system. The appliqués, skirting boards and bars are made of brass and steel.

Manufacturer: **Scavolini**
Photography: **Scavolini**

Rendering

38

The worktops are of black tourmaline quartz with aluminum contours. Quartz is an innovative and highly resistant material.

This renovation project, which included the creation of a dining room, only marginally reduced the space available for the kitchen. In the kitchen, the steel of the electrical appliances and other elements, the granite of the worktop and the black oak of the cupboard doors stand out.

Kazovsky Apartments

Architect: Alla Kazovsky
Location: Nichols Canyon,
Los Angeles, USA
Date of construction: 2007
Photography: Josh Perrin

39

A translucent glass and steel
door was used to separate the
kitchen from the dining room;
when fully open, it visually
connects the two spaces.

The main kitchen of this house was designed to be the backbone of the home. The use of materials like shiny polyester, anodized aluminum and marble enhances the pure and modern style of the rest of the home.

Brentwood Residence

Architect: Belzberg Architects
Location: Brentwood, California, USA
Date of construction: 2007
Photography: Art Gray

40

The appliances and other large elements were placed against the south and east walls so that the kitchen could be used as a passageway between the private and communal areas.

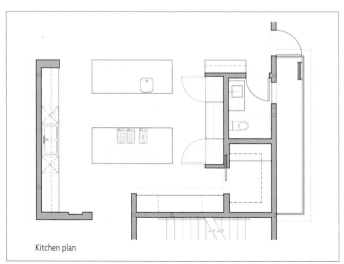

Kitchen plan

The geometric layout of this house includes an almost full circle that surrounds an interior courtyard. In the center of the structure, the living and dining area opens onto the courtyard and landscape.

Contour House

Architect: BKK Architects
Location: Bellarine Peninsula,
Victoria, Australia
Date of construction: 2006
Photography: Shania Shegedyn

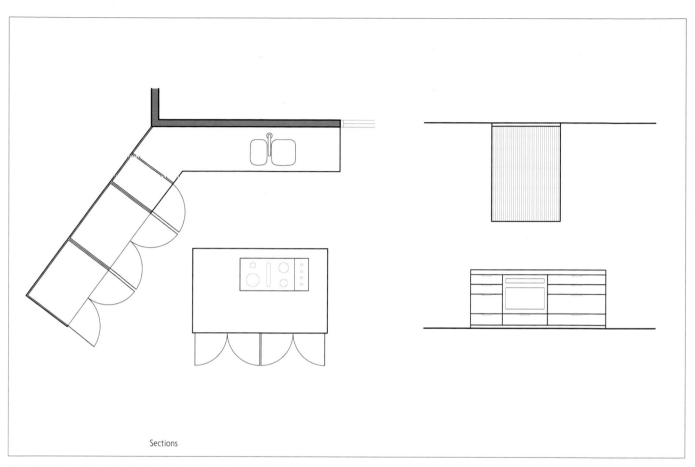

Sections

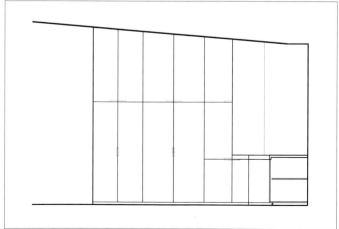

The black cube of the extractor fan signals the kitchen, which is completely integrated into the space.

The concrete used in the central wall surrounding the house has also been used for the worktops in the kitchen.

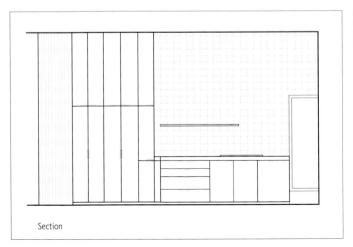

Section

K14 worktops can be cut to fit different spaces with rounded corners and steel-plated aluminum frames. The worktops are available in stone, steel, Corian and Zodiaq, a very resistant material made from quartz.

K14 Collection

Manufacturer: **Boffi**
Photography: **Boffi**

43

The materials used in the surfaces and fronts not only determine the finish, but also the specific uses of the kitchen.

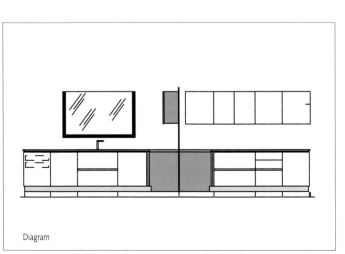

Diagram

© Christophe Pillet

STONE

Inspirations

© Gamadecor

© Christophe Pillet

MIXED MATERIALS

Carmarthen Place

This project involved an extension to a London home in order to convert it into two houses with two separate kitchens, a study and an interior courtyard.

Architect: Emma Doherty & Amanda Menage
Location: London, UK
Date of construction: 2006
Photography: Miran Kambič

44

Although they contrast sharply with the wood that adorns most of the two houses, both the black and white kitchens are integrated into the décor.

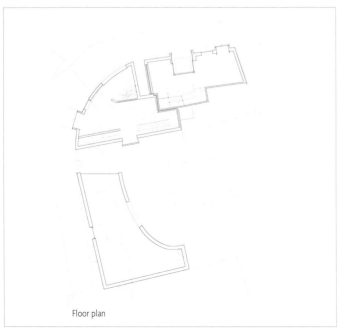

Floor plan

45

In order to make the most of the natural light, the communal areas, including the kitchen, were built on the first floor.

The kitchen was part of an extension to this house. The aim was to harmonize the new areas with the existing ones and to create a minimalist look through the use of noble materials like steel, wood and glass. Different shades of green provide a perfect backdrop.

Meadows House

Architect: Greg Natale Design
Location: Sydney, Australia
Date of construction: 2008
Photography: Sharrin Rees

46

The work table beside the wall in the kitchen continues on the other side of the sliding glass door, forming an outdoor kitchen.

Floor plan

This kitchen was custom designed for the enjoyment of its owners, two passionate cooks, which is why it is in the center of the communal area. It is divided into two parts: a cooking area beside the electrical appliances and a working area in front of this.

Apartment at Ritz Mansions

Architect: Fiona Winzar Architects

Location: Melbourne, Australia

Date of construction: 2005

Photography: Patrick Redmond

47

The island that serves as a worktop is comprised of two mobile elements. It is a modern version of the old French country kitchens and can be moved when necessary.

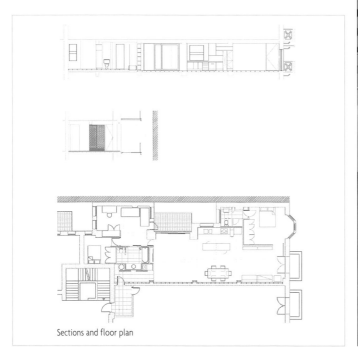

Sections and floor plan

Architect: Arthur Casas
Location: Jacupiranga, Brazil
Date of construction: 2008
Photography: Tuca Reinés

This house is located in Jacupiranga, to the south of São Paulo. In order to make the most of the outdoor space, a small kitchen and dining table were placed on the porch beside the indoor kitchen. The two kitchens are separated by a large sliding window.

48

The large sliding door that separates the kitchen from the outdoor dining room becomes invisible when open and connects the two areas.

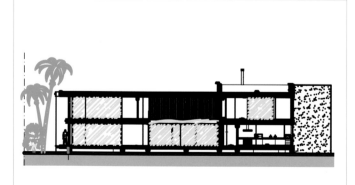

Section

49

The white worktop of the central island and glossy beige wall units allow the natural light entering the kitchen to reflect and reverberate throughout the room.

Located on the hills of Bel Air, this magnificent property was designed by Hal Levitt in the 1960s and was later extended. Simple materials were used in the extension in order to preserve the original essence of the older part of the house.

Casiano Residence

Architect: **Assembledge**
Location: **Los Angeles,
California, USA**
Date of construction: **2006**
Photography: **Assembledge**

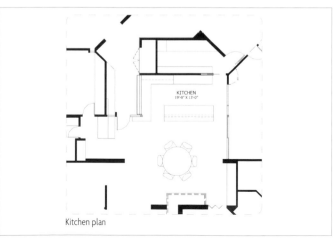

Kitchen plan

50

The wall that separated the kitchen from the dining room was knocked down so that the kitchen—and heart of the home—could open onto the other areas and had the same fantastic views.

Renderings

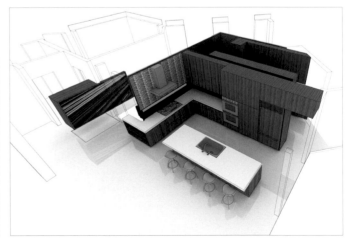

The floors were tiled with terrazzo, and walnut was used in the kitchen cupboards, the same materials that were used in the original building.

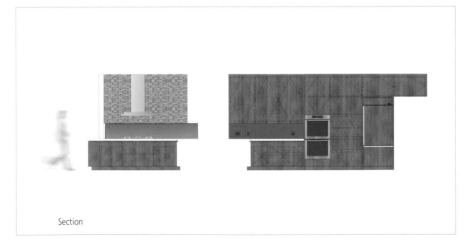

Section

James Robertson House

This house is located on a steep slope to the north of Sydney and surrounded by Ku-ring-gai National Park. The décor includes elements made of glass, steel and copper, which were chosen to blend in with the natural surroundings.

Architect: **Casey Brown**
Location: **Pittwater,
Sydney, Australia**
Date of construction: **2004**
Photography: **Anthony Browell,
Patrick Bingham-Hall**

51

The kitchen and dining room are located on the upper floor and inserted into a glass structure with sliding doors that open onto the outside.

Floor plan

This project is the result of renovating a loft in the heart of NoHo in New York. The steps of the stairs leading to the games room and roof garden are covered in resistant glass, giving the impression that they float over the kitchen.

Alikhani/Petroulas Penthouse

Architect: I-Beam Design
Location: New York, USA
Date of construction: 2005
Photography: Silke Mayer,
Andreas Sterzing

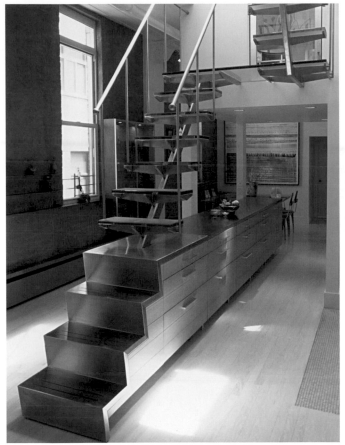

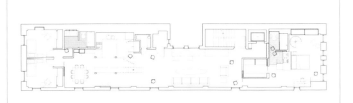

Floor plan

52

The unit constituting the last section of the stairs also serves as storage space for the kitchen and as a worktop. In addition, because it is mobile, it can be used to reach the higher cupboards.

The owner of this home, a cookery book writer, gave the designer, Matali Crasset, carte blanche when redecorating her apartment. Despite the simplicity of the kitchen furniture (by Ikea), the designer successfully used color and other elements to create a unique space that exudes vitality.

Fegh Sgui House

Architect: Matali Crasset
Productions
Location: Paris, France
Date of construction: 2007
Photography: Patrick Gries

53

By using the same color scheme in the wall of the kitchen and the dining table, the designer has created a link between the two areas and visual consistency.

Drawing

Glass is the focal point of this renovation project, where the aim was to make the patio behind the kitchen and bathroom visible from the main door using glass and a mirror.

Semann Slattery Kitchen

Architect: Greg Natale
Location: Darlington, Australia
Date of construction: 2003
Photography: Sharrin Rees

54

The use of a mirror with a chrome plated metal frame in the kitchen is quite a novel idea. The mirror reflects the patio just behind, making it look like it is part of the interior.

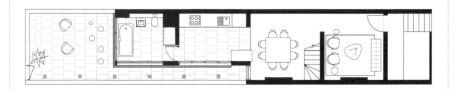

Floor plan

Guangzhou Show House

The aim when designing this kitchen was to create a clear link between the kitchen and the lounge. The small set of steps creates a spatial and visual separation. The kitchen at the end of the room is visible, although partially hidden by the partition wall.

Architect: One Plus Partnership
Location: Guangzhou, China
Date of construction: 2007
Photography: Law Ling Kit,
Virginia Lung

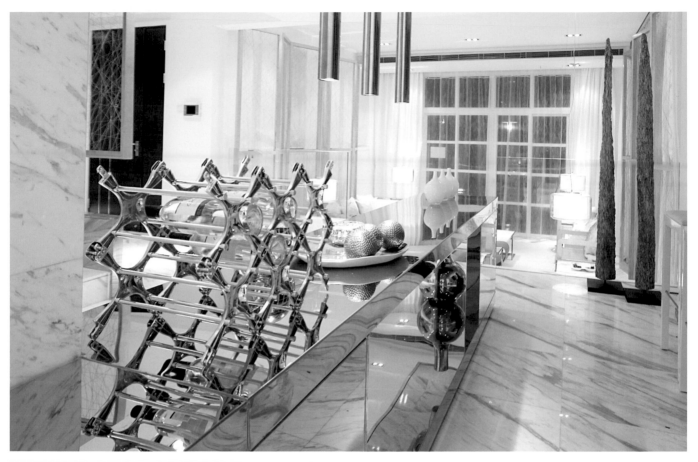

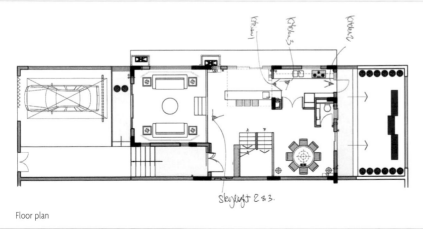

Floor plan

55

At the entrance to the kitchen, the low mirror unit denotes the access point, whereas a taller panel would have created the impression of a passageway.

This kitchen is comprised of three large and clearly differentiated areas consisting of a central island, an extractor fan and a furniture unit with the TV, which opens onto the dining area.

Apartment in Sant Lluís Street

Architect: Air Projects/ Raúl Campderrich
Location: Barcelona, Spain
Date of construction: 2005
Photography: Jordi Miralles

56

A large island separates the working and eating areas of this kitchen. The shiny black wood contrasts with the polished steel surfaces.

This home is laid out around a large lacquered wood module that runs the length of the house. In the kitchen area at the center of the house, the module acts as a rear wall and contains the electrical appliances and storage space.

Penthouse in Stuttgart

Architect: Raiser Lopes Designers
Location: Stuttgart, Germany
Date of construction: 2007
Photography: Frank Kleinbach

57

In the center of the living room, the boundaries of the kitchen are defined using a block with a glazed glass table top, which contains the cooking and washing areas.

Section and floor plan

Different floor levels are used to separate the different areas. A small step leads to the kitchen. On either side of the central island and against the walls, we have the different kitchen appliances. Just behind, and on a slightly higher level, we have the dining room.

Three levels loft

Architect: Carreté Gelpí
Arquitectes
Location: Barcelona, Spain
Date of construction: 2002
Photography: Jordi Miralles

Situated in Beverly Hills, this house has marvelous views of San Francisco Valley. Because it opens onto the terrace, garden and lounge, it receives plenty of natural light and is the nerve center of the home.

Brosmith Residence

Architect: SPF:architects
Location: Beverly Hills,
California, USA
Date of construction: 2004
Photography: John Linden

58

The kitchen is located in the center of the house and is organized into segments in accordance with the different functions: cooking, washing and eating.

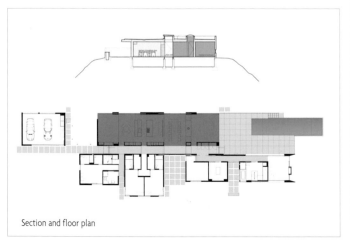

Section and floor plan

The Flux Collection by Scavolini presents various circular solutions with lacquered finishes. Technology, innovative design, ergonomics, flexibility and multifunctionality are the trademarks of this new line.

Scavolini Flux

Manufacturer: **Scavolini**
Photography: **Scavolini**

59

This innovative circular island is extremely comfortable and has the capacity to hold all of the essential kitchen utensils and accessories.

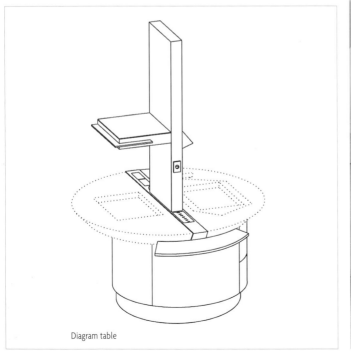

Diagram table

Diagram circular table

60

The circular cooking area in the corner includes a cupboard with a rotating basket to optimise storage space and to have everything on hand.

Zone Collection

Manufacturer: **Boffi**
Photography: **Boffi**

Boffi's Zone modules are combined with the basic elements of this brand. This piece, which can be converted into an island, includes a pull-out glass worktop that doubles up as a table or work area.

61

The embedded handles that open by pressure create even door surfaces in different stainless steel finishes.

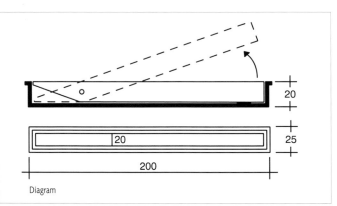

Diagram

This kitchen was designed so as to allow access from several points. A partition was erected in the main room to house the kitchen, and the games area receives plenty of natural light thanks to an overhead skylight.

Pattison Road House

Architect: SHH Architects
Location: London, UK
Date of construction: 2005
Photography: SHH Architects

62

The kitchen, which also serves as a casual dining room, can be concealed at any time with the sliding doors.

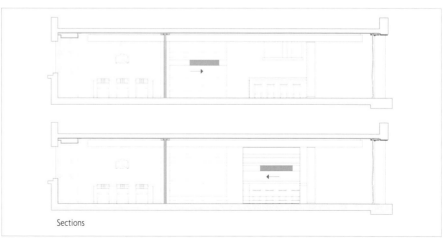

Sections

63

When the doors are closed, the small rectangular window in one of the panels enables the person inside to watch the TV or to see what is going on outside.

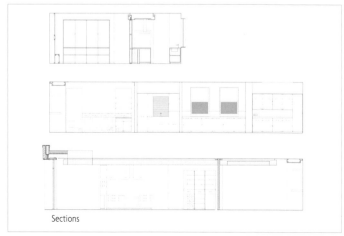

Sections

Flash House

This kitchen, accessible from the stairs and terrace, receives plenty of natural light and is separated from the living room by a large fireplace. Because of its privileged location, it can afford to play with different materials, finally choosing shiny black polyester for the modules.

Architect: **Filippo Bombace**
Location: **Rome, Italy**
Date of construction: **2006**
Photography: **Luigi Filetici**

64

A daring choice of materials: steel surfaces and black lacquered furniture stand out against pink velvet upholstery.

Longitudinal section

C.E.D.V. House

Although this kitchen is a separate unit, it is connected to the living room via a large opening between the wall units and the working area. The blue of the fabrics and painted tiles (by Viteri) visually connects the different areas.

Architect: **Filippo Bombace**
Location: **Rome, Italy**
Date of construction: **2003**
Photography: **Luigi Filetici**

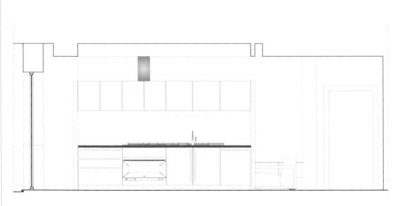
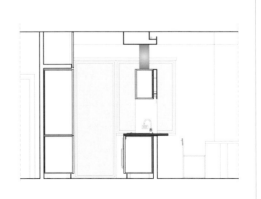

Sections

65

Roller blinds hide the kitchen and the electrical appliances are partly concealed by fiber curtains.

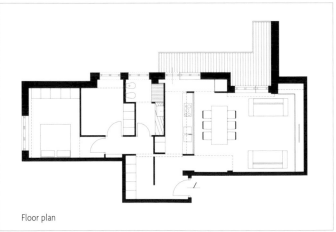

Floor plan

This compact wall-closet runs the length of the kitchen until becoming a shelf in the adjoining room. The kitchen is comprised of two levels; the lower level is used by the whole family and the upper level is a private area connected to the lower level with a ladder hidden behind the unit.

Architect: Fuhrimann and Hächler Architekten
Location: Zurich, Germany
Date of construction: 2006
Photography: Valentin Jeck

66

The main material used is
MDM, which has been
worked into curved shapes
reminiscent of the
architectural language of
Brazilian Modernism.

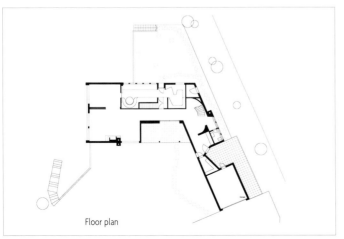

Floor plan

Canonbury Grove

The focal point of this project is a three-dimensional wooden piece that defines the different areas, while directing the dynamics of the space. Solid sucupira wood denotes the warm areas for cooking and eating, and the suspended back-lit ceiling frames the piece.

Architect: SCAPE Architects
Location: London, UK
Date of construction: 2005
Photography: Kilian O'Sullivan

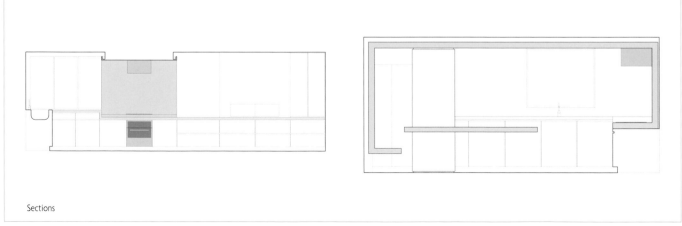

Sections

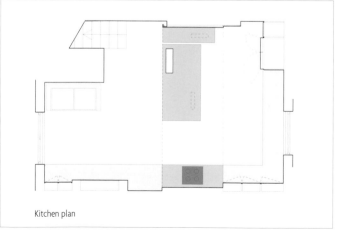

Kitchen plan

67

The wooden breakfast bar in this kitchen not only provides additional work space and a table for quick meals; it is also a subtle element denoting the space devoted to the kitchen.

This kitchen was designed in an open-plan style in order to integrate it into the other rooms and to make the most of the natural light. The doors of the units in the main panel are of wengé veneer.

Penthouse in Andorra

Architect: Arteks Arquitectura
Location: Andorra La Vella
Date of construction: 2003
Photography: Eugeni Pons

68

The kitchen units are framed
with dichroic lamps and the
entire piece was built in
the direction of the arched
ceiling.

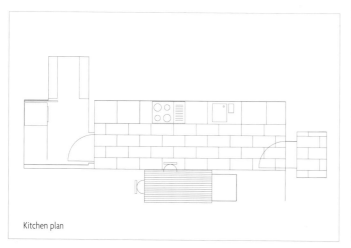

Kitchen plan

69

The central island has an in-built sliding table that glides over the surface when needed and can be stowed out of sight when not in use.

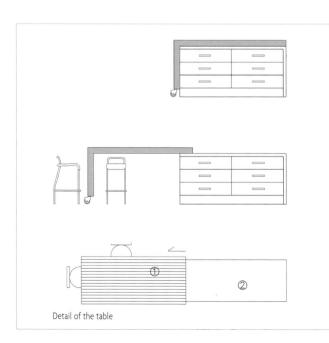

Detail of the table

Lovers of the culinary arts always prefer solid, timeless pieces in heavy wood, but with sophisticated finishes. The Yara series is a perfect example of how to combine high technology with the warmth and timelessness of wood.

Yara Collection

Manufacturer: **Cesar Cucine**
Photography: **Cesar Cucine**

70

Straight lines and even wood finishes characterize this collection which shuns unnecessary details, without losing its functionality.

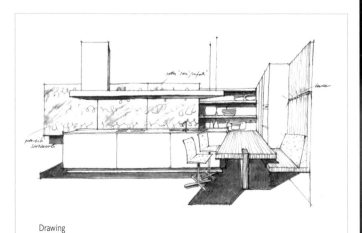

Drawing

© Binova

MIXED MATERIALS

Inspirations

oliform USA

© Mobalco

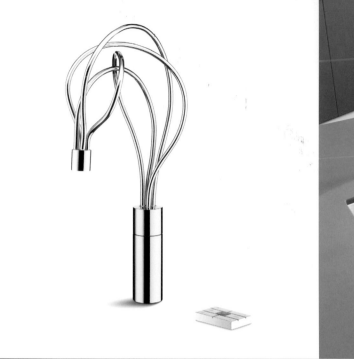

DESIGN CODE

© Sheer

COMPACT KITCHENS

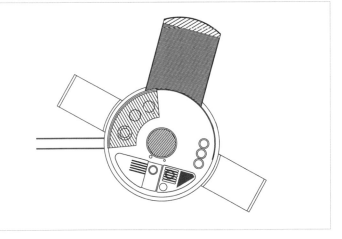

71

This compact kitchen has all the essential elements of a kitchen, including hobs, a sink and even a pull-out table. The main materials used are carbon fiber, steel and Corian.

© Artificio

72

This island is comprised of cubes that are vertically and randomly suspended from the worktop. The feeling of weightlessness is due to the fact that they are only supported by two central legs.

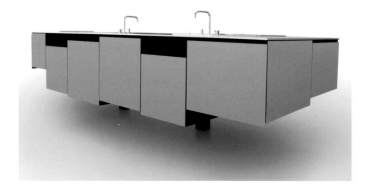

© Artificio

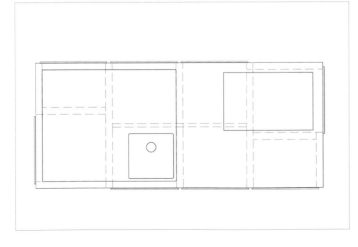

73

The storage block in this module contains the fridge, cold cupboard, freezer and hot cupboard, all in a single piece that plays with the different color panels.

© Boffi

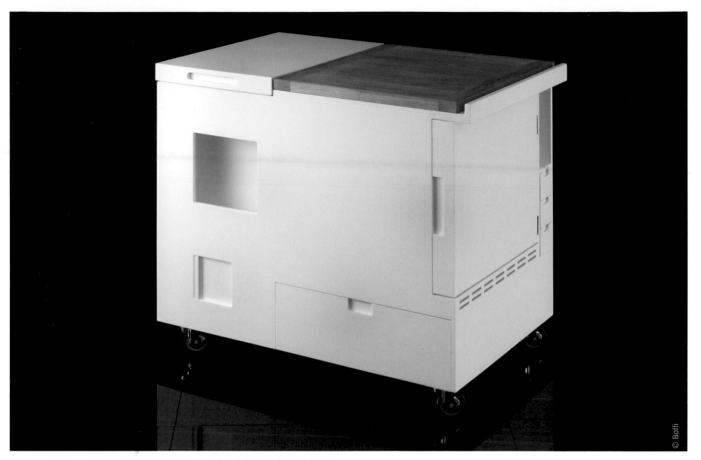

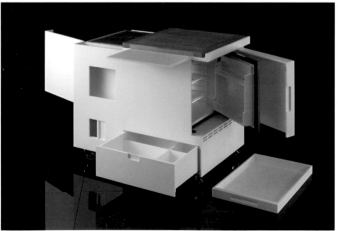

© Boffi

74

The Minikitchen is a new version of the kitchen that Joe Colombo designed for Boffi in 1963. It is made of Corian and has induction cooktops; a box on wheels that performs all the necessary functions.

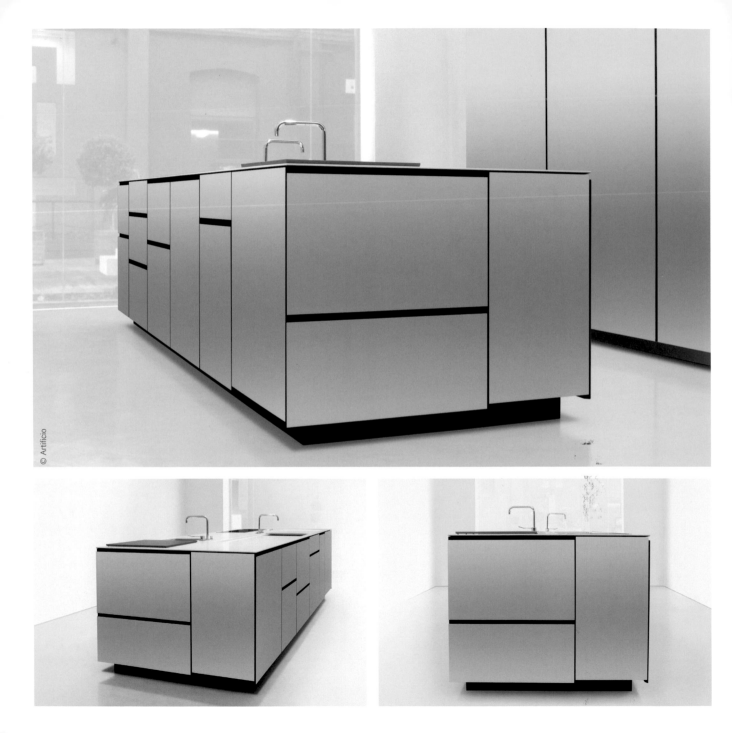

© Electrolux

75

Let us not forget that kitchens can also be built outdoors, often in the form of a barbecue or broiler. This barbecue by Electrolux runs on coal and includes all the essential elements in a small space.

76

Just by pulling out the table, chairs and lamp, this flat image becomes a 3D kitchen. The door of the upper unit folds horizontally to reveal the worktops and storage space.

77

The Arcus stove concept lets you turn up the heat with a simple twist of the pan, and the adjustable tempered glass panel isolates the steam and prevents splashing.

© Rieber

78

The circular design of the Rieber Waterstation enables it to rotate 360 degrees on its axis. In addition to having a sink, it also includes all types of accessories for cooking and other optional items.

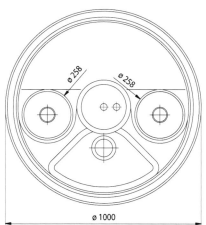

ø 258   ø 258

ø 1000

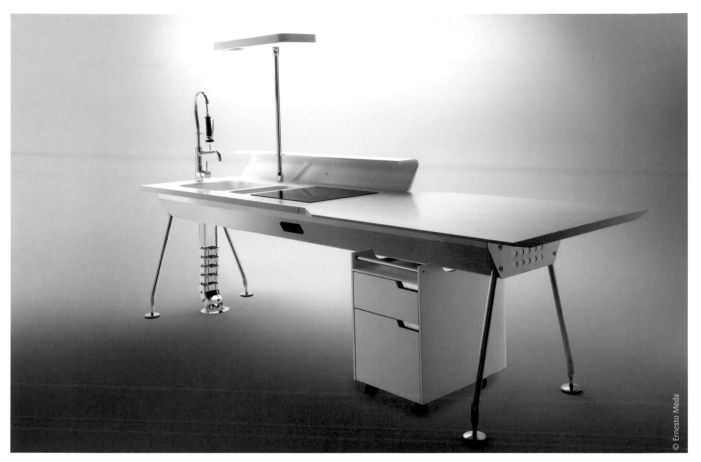

© Ernesto Meda

79

This kitchen consists of a large white Corian table with steel legs. On one side we have a vitroceramic hob and sink, and on the other the worktop, which can also be used as a desk.

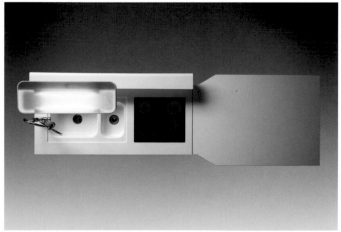

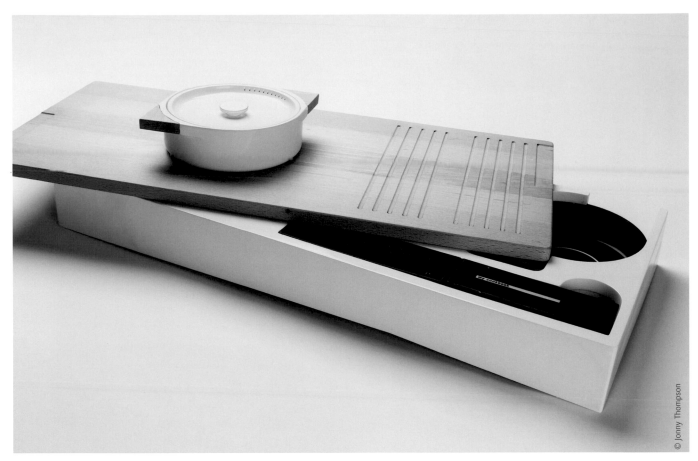

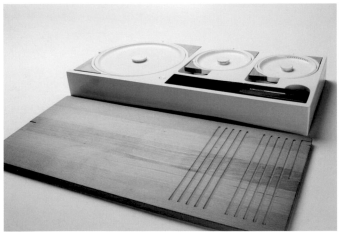

80

One solution for small kitchens is the Single Person Cooker, which is a box containing cooking utensils and accessories, chopping boards and even a wok.

81

The sliding door of this kitchen allows you to hide some of the contents. It includes all the essential elements, including large cupboards that come in a variety of finishes and colors to match the rest of the décor.

82

This model is an ecological kitchen that is capable of taking care of the plants so you can make vegetable soap. The top part is a biological garden and spices and the lower part contains a cooker and sink.

83

Coox is a multipurpose kitchen on wheels that includes three hobs and a pull-out work surface. The height can be adjusted, and when the hobs are switched off it doubles up as a side table.

EXTRACTOR HOODS

84

This hood takes up the whole length of the lower kitchen island. On the one side we have the extractor over the hob, and the rest of the space can be used as a shelf for spices or kitchenware.

© Elica

© Elica

© Dada

© Elica

85

In addition to the traditional extractor hoods, there are a whole range of inconspicuous models available to blend in with the rest of the décor.

86

Kitchens with stand-alone cooktops require suspended extractor hoods. There are a range of finishes and designs to choose from to suit every kitchen.

© Elica

87

If you are looking for as light and ethereal a piece as possible, a good option is a translucent glass base in place of models made of steel or other opaque materials.

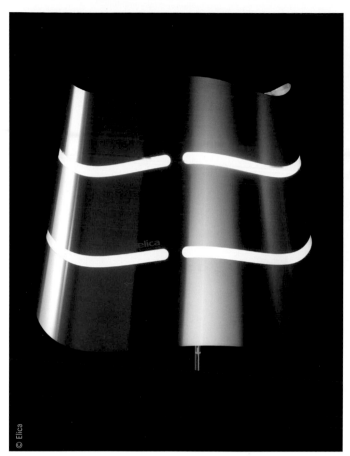

88

This hood by Elica Stone Gallery is completely hidden by a front panel made of stone and lit with one or two adjustable lamps.

89

Stainless steel is one of the most popular materials for use in extractor hoods. In addition to being resistant and durable, its color and light reflecting surface looks elegant in any kitchen.

© Kohler

SINKS

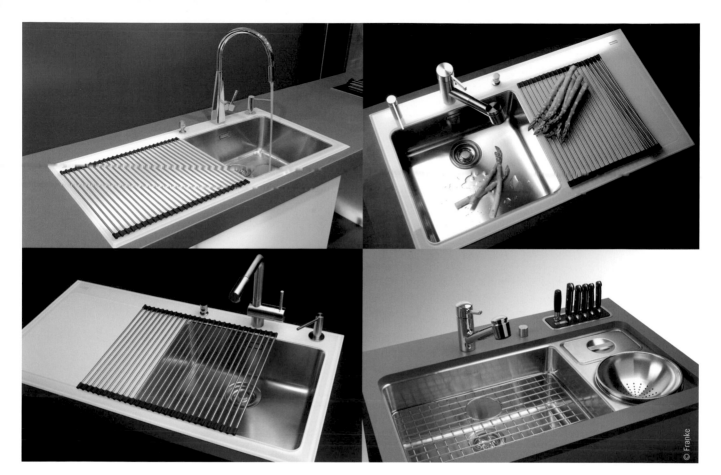

90

Some sinks are designed to hold chopping boards so that you can conveniently wash food in the sink while preparing food.

91

Another practical way of washing and straining food is to use grating that slides into place under the faucet.

92

Accessories like baskets and trays can be attached to the sink, enabling you to conveniently wash the food or soak the different utensils while you cook.

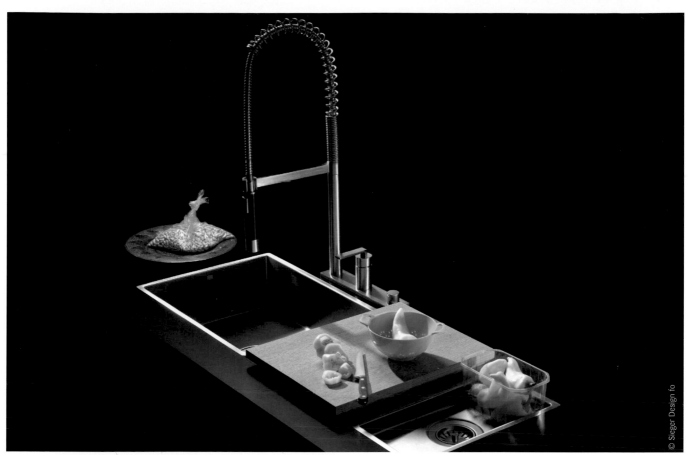

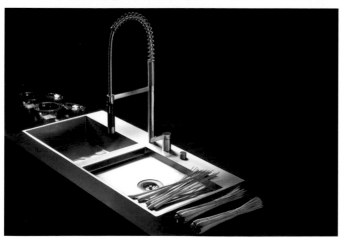

93

These sinks by Dorbracht serve a dual purpose. On the one hand you have the sink, and beside it a space for preparing the food beside a small ledge.

© Kohler

© Nativetrails

94

In addition to the standard round, square or slightly rectangular sinks; you can find several different designs with original shapes to give your kitchen a touch of personality.

© Kohler

© Nativetrails

© Kohler

95

The unusual Luna model by Nativetrails represents a new concept in sinks. It has two drains, one on either side of the basin.

96

The materials most commonly used in worktops are marble, Silestone, wood and stainless steel. In this case, glass has been used to create a very interesting contrast with wood.

97

Innovative materials have been invented for use in worktops and come in eye-catching colors like orange, which is no less resistant or durable.

© Sonoma Stone

98

This glass covers the sink to keep it immaculately clean and can also be used as a chopping board for food.

© Franke

© Franke

© Binova

Stainless steel is still the preferred choice of material for kitchens. Its durability and resistance to corrosion make it an ideal material for sinks, faucets, electrical appliances and all kinds of kitchenware.

© Dornbracht

FAUCETS

© MGS Designs

© Dornbracht

— 100 —

Faucets with high spouts are much more practical for kitchen sinks. Because of their height, it is easy to wash all types of kitchen utensils, even the largest of items.

— 101 —

Faucets with rounded shapes and wide curved spouts are the height of elegance and style.

© Newform

102

With single-handle faucets, it is easier to turn on the tap, and the flow and mixture of hot and cold water can be adjusted with just one hand.

© Arwa

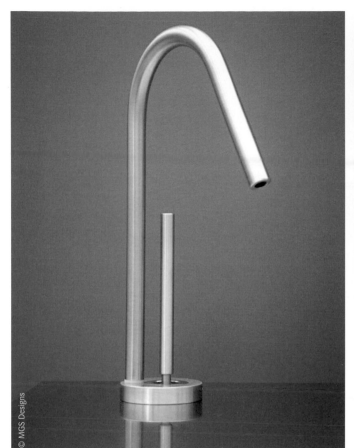

© MGS Designs

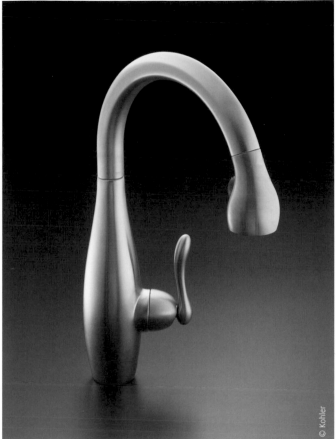

© Kohler

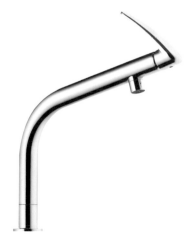

© Dada

A wide variety of single-handle systems are now available; some can even be inserted into the bottom of the sink or at the end, beside the water outlet.

104

Having boiling water readily at hand at all times is now possible with Quooker, a faucet that is connected to an electric water heater that heats the water to boiling point.

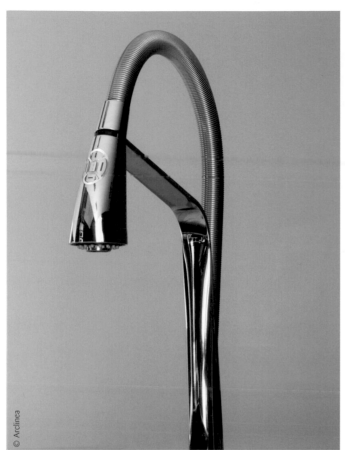

105

The Karbon articulating kitchen faucet by Kohler is engineered to hold any pose for hands-free operation, and comes with different water jets.

© Newform

The Y-Con model by Newform
has a temperature sensor and
a LED that signals different
shades of red and blue
depending on the water
temperature.

107

Faucets with straight-angle spouts give the kitchen a masculine feel because of their clean-cut and rigid form.

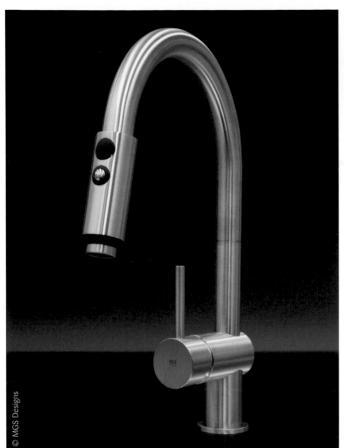

© MGS Designs

© Arclinea

108

Apart from the standard faucet, other mechanisms are also available to activate the flow of water, such as sensors that turn on a water jet that is hidden in the sink.

109

This faucet by Kohler has an articulated and turnable spout. It extends from the sink to other parts of the worktop for different uses. When not needed, it can be neatly folded up and takes up very little space.

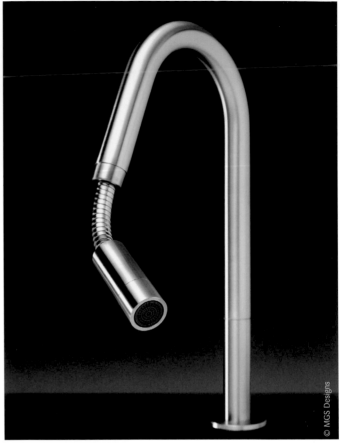

110

Extractable or extendible
spouts are very practical, as
are the steerable nozzles that
allow you to direct the water
jet in the desired direction.

111

The Twinflex faucet by Arwa has a totally flexible spout that can be positioned in different ways. With an eye-catching design and chrome finish, it comes in four different colors: orange, gray, blue and black.

© Newform

112

Faucets are also available in white and the D-Rect model by Newform has a white lacquered finish and a minimalist design.

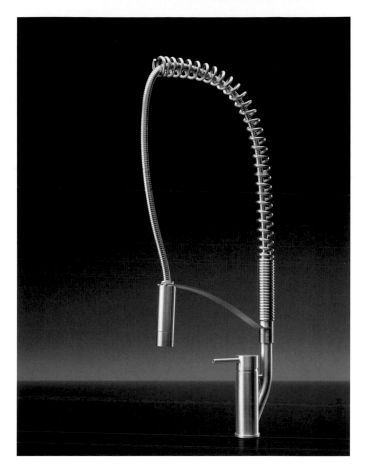

113

In some cases, faucets are authentic works of art for serious rooms like the kitchen, coming with uniquely shaped spouts that resemble sculptures.

STORAGE

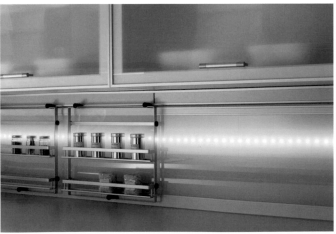

114

Closets with sliding doors are a clever way to save space because the hinged-angle required to open the door of a standard closet is not required.

115

Corner units are difficult to access, but there are a number of alternatives, such as swivel and pull-out shelves that provide access to all the utensils at a single touch.

116

At first glance, these drawers look quite normal, but actually convert into a dining table and two benches. When folded, they can be conveniently stored in the kitchen unit.

117

Because it has no handles, the stainless steel cupboard at the end of the kitchen island is inconspicuous and looks like just another decorative detail.

118

Storage cupboards and spaces behind the worktop are very useful because they provide easy and convenient access to all the kitchen utensils.

© Dica

119

There are lots of ways to create additional storage space without foregoing aesthetics. One option is to suspend a structure from the ceiling to hang pots and pans.

© Alno

120

The insides of closets can be
designed to serve different
functions. This small dishwasher
has been built into and hidden
between the other cupboards
and the door matches the other
doors in the unit.

© Alno

© Yael Pincus

121

Drawers of different heights can easily be used to store all types of utensils and products, from kitchenware to food.

© Binova

122

Small corner units can be added to any space to store the different utensils. This drawer is a useful way to neatly store your herb and spice jars.

© Rational

© Fagor

© Performa

123

The doors of wall units that open horizontally to the left or right are now being replaced with vertical doors, which are much more convenient.

124

The handles of this silverware tray enable it to be easily pulled out when placing the different pieces behind the sink or setting the table.

125

This small spice rack has been built into the wall unit and can be pulled out at a single touch, ensuring that the seasonings are readily at hand when cooking.

© Arclinea

© Balvi

126

Trolley tables are very useful in kitchens with sufficient space. These can be rolled around as needed and even double up as a side table for the dining room when necessary.

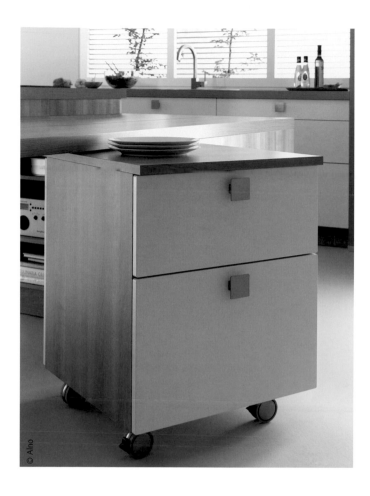

© Aïno

© Vinçon

127

These items are very useful for storing kitchenware or food and can even be used as a fruit holder, for example. They are sometimes designed in the form of a kitchen unit and trolley and have drawers and cupboards.

© Jordi Miralles

BIG IDEAS

© Jordi Miralles

128

One way of achieving a more casual look and hiding the cold surfaces of electrical appliances and cupboards is to use panels. There is a wide variety of designs, photographs and drawings to choose from.

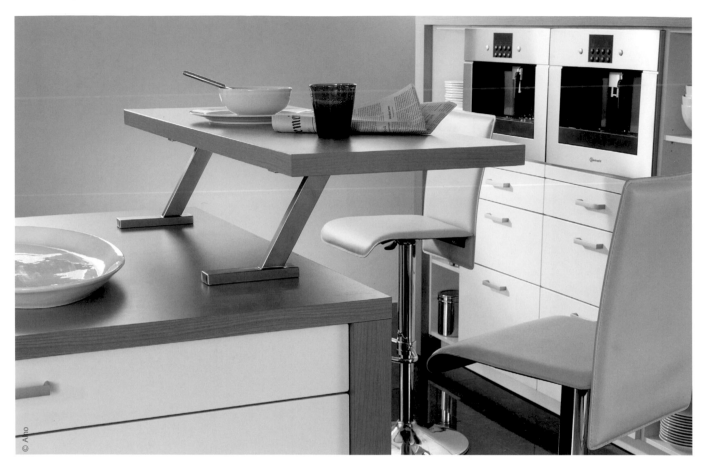

129

To make the most of the space and to create a breakfast area in the kitchen, a small, slightly raised extension can be added to the side of the island or the end of the kitchen unit.

© Alno

Work comfortably in the kitchen or take a break from standing with this auxiliary chair from the MyWay collection by Alno, which can be pulled out of the closet with a mere pull of the handle.

131

A piece of slate in the kitchen enables you to jot down recipes or the shopping list. Devices that can be hung from the utensil rails are available to hold the cookery book while you cook.

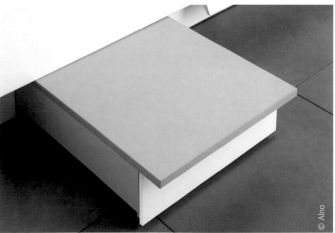

132

Several designs are available to make household chores easier: sliding doors to separate rooms, chopping boards with a hole and a garbage can underneath, and small pull-out steps to reach the high cupboards.

© Yael Pincus

ACCESSORIES

© Bulthaup

133

Chopping boards are an essential item for any kitchen. A very practical option is a large board that is built into the worktop to keep it steady and immobile.

GEMÜSE | VEGETABLES | LEGUMES

FISCH | FISH | POISSON

© Konstantin

134

There are a wide range of boards on the market in a variety of materials, such as wood, nylon, polyester, bamboo and resin

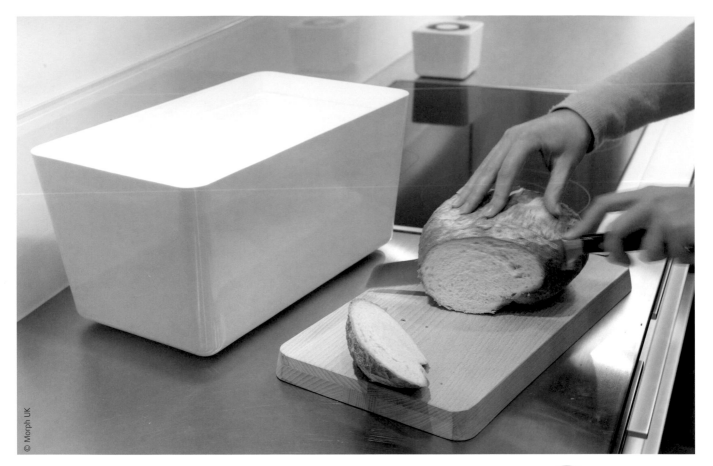

135

This stylish and eye-catching bread box keeps the bread fresh and the wooden lid doubles up as a bread board.

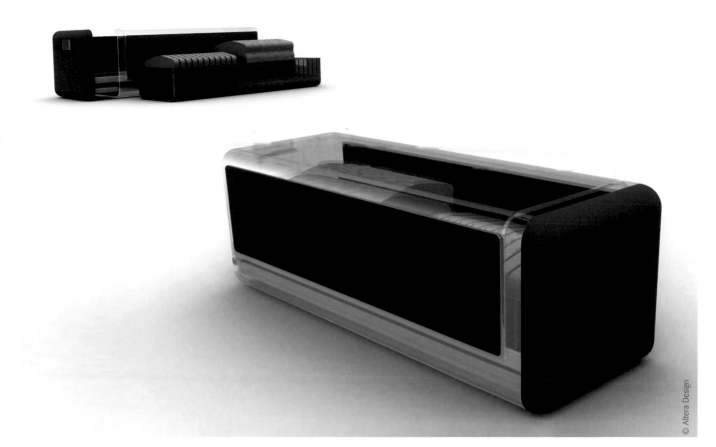

© Altera Design

136

Cortar, servir y conservar. Son las tres funciones que realiza Tekmek, una panera con una ranura por donde se introduce el cuchillo para cortar el pan y una bandeja extraíble para servirlo en la mesa.

137

Los electrodomésticos también pueden servir para modernizar la cocina. Además de prácticos, los electrodomésticos con diseños divertidos y llamativos confieren personalidad a la estancia.

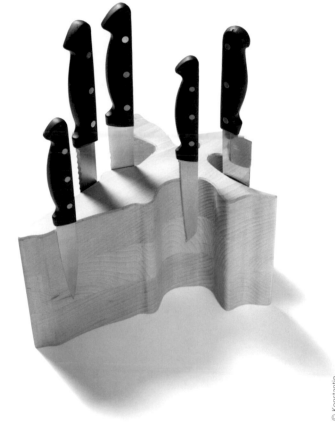

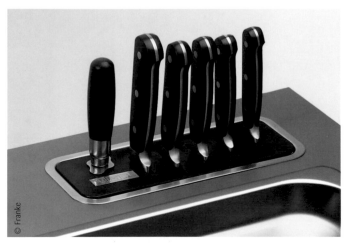

© Franke

© Konstantin

138

Los cuchillos son la herramienta básica en la cocina y conviene tenerlos siempre bien a mano. Algunos diseñadores añaden un pequeño hueco en el fregadero donde colocarlos.

© Siematic

© Vinçon

© Conran

139

Además de los botelleros, cada vez es más habitual encontrar en las cocinas pequeños conservadores de vino y cava, e incluso neveras que incorporan un espacio para estos refrigeradores.

© Siematic

140

A la hora de cocinar resulta muy práctico tener a mano todos los utensilios básicos. Los rieles, que se colocan en la pared, permiten colgar todo tipo de cacharros y accesorios.

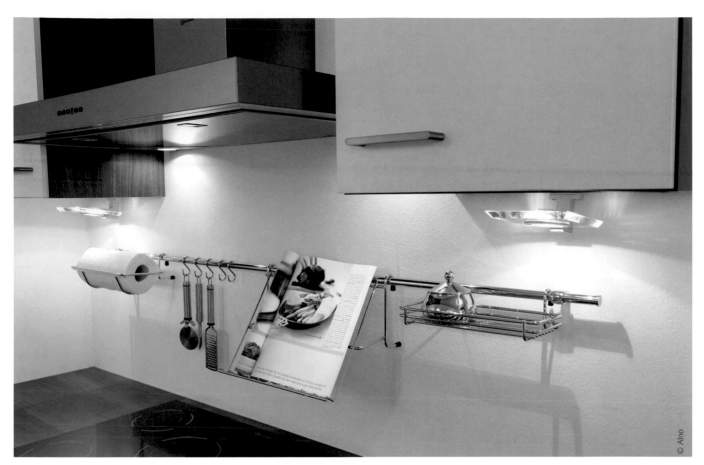

© Alno

© Iittala Group

Accesorios **583**

142

Aunque los coladores ya están incluidos en muchas baterías de cocina, podemos encontrar modelos de plástico con un diseño más actual, originales formas y llenos de colorido.

143

Con el fin de ahorrar espacio, algunos de coladores son plegables. Están formados por círculos concéntricos que se pliegan hasta convertirse en un pequeño objeto plano y fácil de guardar.

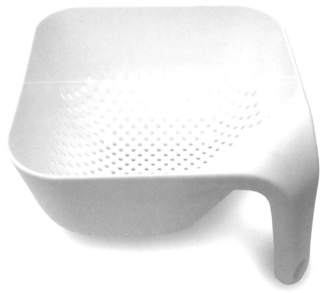

144

Esta original y divertida pieza es un medidor de raciones de espaguetis. Cada uno de los círculos corresponde a una cantidad diferente, lo que permite acertar siempre con la ración adecuada.

145

Cualquier cocinero que se precie siempre cuenta con una amplia variedad de condimentos y especias. Se pueden guardar en pequeños botes sobre estantes que se cuelgan junto a los fogones.

146

Table mats are a kitchen necessity. Although most worktops are now made of resistant materials, an extra table mat never goes amiss.

147

Steel is the most common material for cookware sets, especially pots and pans. This particular model was inspired by the old wrought iron saucepans with wooden handles.

148

Bialetti's Spazio System includes a large number of pieces with handles that open in one flick and fold onto the sides, enabling you to save storage space.

149

One of the most useful
cooking accessories is a
spoon to support the utensils
while you cook, allowing you
to keep the worktop
spotlessly clean.

150

Novel pieces, such as this juicer designed by Philippe Starck or the angel and devil salt and pepper set combine functionality and style.

Directory

Acn+ Architektur
Schopenhauerstrasse 19/2/15
1180 Vienna, Austria
P. +43 1 968 27 63
office@acnplus.at

Adela Cabré (interior design)
Diputació 229
08007 Barcelona, Spain
P. +34 93 453 33 31
adela@adelacabreinteriorismo.com
www.adelacabreinteriorismo.com

Air Projects/Raúl Campderrich
Pau Claris 179, 3, 1
08037 Barcelona, Spain
P. +34 93 272 24 27
info@air-projects.com
www.air-projects.com

Alex Bradley Design
info@alexbradleydesign.co.uk
www.alexbradleydesign.co.uk
Single Person Cooker

Alla Kazovsky
1853 Nichols Canyon Road
Los Angeles, CA 90046, USA
P. +1 323 436 0286

Altera Design Studio
Asiagieglence Mestan Sokak 12-15
Etlik 06010, Ankara, Turkey
P. +90 312 321 82 39
info@alt-era.com
www.alt-era.com

Antoine Lebrun
info@antoinelebrun.fr
www.antoinelebrun.fr
Coox (collaboration with Fagor)

Argemí Falguera Arquitectura
Passeig Manuel Girona 60, ático
08034 Barcelona, Spain
P. +34 93 205 47 30
www.argemi-falguera.com

Arteks Arquitectura
Unió 1, 1ª-A
500 Andorra La Vella, Andorra
P. +376 805 205
info@arteks.ad
www.arteksarquitectura.com

Arthur Casas
Rua Capivari 160
Pacaembu, São Paulo, Brazil
P. +55 11 2182 7500
casas@arthurcasas.com.br
www.arthurcasas.com.br

Assembledge
6363 Wilshire Boulevard, 401
Los Angeles, CA 90048, USA
P. +1 323 951 0045
dt@assembledge.com
ks@assembledge.com
www.assembledge.com

Belzberg Architects
1501 Colorado Ave., Suite B
Santa Monica, 90401 CA, USA
P. +1 310 453 9611
info@belzbergarchitects.com
www.belzbergarchitects.com

BKK Architects
Level 9, 180 Russell St
Melbourne 3000, Victoria, Australia
T: +613 9671 4555
office@b-k-k.com.au
www.b-k-k.com.au

Carolina Nisivoccia
Via Giasone del Maino 20
20146 Milano, Italy
P. +39 02 4390815
info@nisivoccia-architettura.com
www.nisivoccia-architettura.com

Carreté Gelpí Arquitectes
Avinguda de Vallvidrera 69, bajos
08017 Barcelona, Spain
P. +34 93 418 64 47
admin@cga.cat
www.cga.cat

Casey Brown Architecture
Level 1, 63 William Street
East Sydney NSW 2010, Australia
P. +61 2 9360 7977
cb@caseybrown.com.au
www.caseybrown.com.au

Centrala Designers Task Force
P. +48 602 316 374
szczesny@centrala.net.pl
www.centrala.net.pl

Christophe Pillet
Agence Christophe Pillet
29, pasaje Dubail, 75010 Paris, France
P. +33 158 36 46 31
info@christophepillet.com
www.christophepillet.com

Emma Doherty & Amanda Menage
76 Bermondsey Street
London SE1 3UP, UK
P. +44 7961 123 074
amanda@bstreetstudio.co.uk
www.bstreetstudio.co.uk

Filippo Bombace
1, Via Monte Tomatico
00141 Rome, Italy
P. +39 06 868 98266
info@filippobombace.com
www.filippobombace.com

Fiona Winzar Architects
1.03/129 Fitzroy Street, The George
St Kilda VIC 3182, Australia
P. +61 3 9593 6464
fiona@winzar-architects.com.au
www.winzar-architects.com.au

Fuhrimann and Hächler Architekten
Hardturmstrasse 66
8005 Zürich, Switzerland
P. +41 44 271 04 80
mail@afgh.ch
www.afgh.ch

Greg Natale Design
Studio 6 Level 3, 35 Buckingham Street
Surry Hills NSW 2010, Australia
P. +61 2 8399 2103
info@gregnatale.com
www.gregnatale.com

Hiroaki Ohtani
4-11-4 Himoyamate-dori, Chuo-ku
Kobe 650-0011, Japan
ootani@nikken.ko.jp

I-Beam Design
245 West 29th St. Suite 501A
New York, NY 10001, USA
P. +34 212 244 7597
suzan@i-beamdesign.com
azin@i-beamdesign.com
www.i-beamdesign.com

i29 Interior Architects
Industrieweg 29
1115 AD Duivendrecht,
The Netherlands
P. +20 695 61 20
info@i29.nl
www.i29.nl

Ian Moore Architects
85 Mclachlan Ave, Rushcutters Bay
Sydney, NSW 2011 Australia
P. +61 2 93 80 4099
info@ianmoorearchitects.com
www.ianmoorearchitects.com

Ibarra Rosano Design Architects
2849 East Sylvia Street
Tucson, AZ 85716, USA
P. +1 520 795 5477
mail@ibarrarosano.com
www.ibarrarosano.com

Jordi Galí & Estudi
Passatge Forasté 4, entresuelo D
08022 Barcelona, Spain
P. +34 932 115 442
jg@jgaliestudi.com
www.jgaliestudi.com

Julie Brion & Tanguy Leclercq
154 Avenue Circulaire
1180 Brussels, Belgium
P. +32 2 640 00 18
bl@brionleclercq.com
www.brionleclercq.com

Klumpp & Klumpp Architekten
Im Grörach 12
72631 Aichtal, Germany
P. 07127 953500

Lizarriturry Tuneu
Castell 6
17256 Palau Sator, Girona, Spain
P. +972 634 119
lita@coac.net
www.lizarriturry.com/arquitectura

Manuel Perez Prada
Adalbert-Stifter-Weg 6,
97299 Zell a.M., Germany
mpp_design@yahoo.de
www.perezprada.com
Cooperation with Mièle & Cie. KG

Markus Wespi & Jérôme de Meuron
Architects
Caviano + Zürich
6578 Caviano, Switzerland
P. +41 91 794 17 73
info@wespidemeuron.ch
www.wespidemeuron.ch

Matali Crasset Productions
26 rue du Buisson Saint Louis
F-75010 Paris, France
P. +33 1 42 40 99 89
matali.crasset@wanadoo.fr
www.matalicrasset.com

Melanie Olle and Ilja Oelschägel
ilja.oelschlaegel@burg-halle.de
Grandma's Revenge Project
Photos: Nicolaus Brade

Nieberg Architect
Waterloostrasse 1
30169 Hannover, Germany
P. +49 511 169 6601
mail@nieberg-architect.de
www.nieberg-architect.de

One Plus Partnership Limited
4/F, 332 Lockhart Road
Wanchai, Hong Kong, China
P. +852 2591 9308
admin@onepluspartnership.com
www.onepluspartnership.com

Pb Elemental Architecture
1916 23rd Ave. South
Seattle, WA 98144, USA
P. +1 206 285 1464
info@elementalarchitecture.com
www.elementalarchitecture.com

Pensando en blanco/Aurora Polo,
Borja Garmendia
Fraxkueneko Murrua 2, bajo
20280 Hondarribia, Gipuzcoa, Spain
P. +943 642 551
info@pensandoenblanco.com
www.pensandoenblanco.com

Pierre Hebbelinck Atelier
d'Architecture
41-43 Rue Fond Pirette
4000 Liege, Belgium
P. +32 4 226 53 26
atelier@pierrehebbelinck.net
www.pierrehebbelinck.net

Project Orange
2nd Floor, Block E, Morelands, 5-23
Old Street
EC1V 9HL London, UK
P. +44 0207 566 0410
mail@projectorange.com
www.projectorange.com

Raiser Lopes Designers
Hauptmannsreute 69
D-70193 Stuttgart, Germany
P. +49 711 248 3919
www.raiserlopes.com

Samsó & Associats
Tallers 77, ático
08001 Barcelona, Spain
P. +34 93 412 12 43

SCAPE Architects
Unit 2 Providence Yard
Off Ezra Street
E2 7RJ London, UK
P. +44 20 7012 1244
mail@scape-architects.com
www.scape-architects.com

SHH Architects
1 Vencourt Place, Ravenscourt Park
Hammersmith
London, W6 9NU, UK
P. +44 020 8600 4171
info@shh.co.uk
www.shh.co.uk

Sieger Design GmbH & Co. KG
Schloss Harkotten
48336 Sassenberg, Germany
P. +49 54 26/94 92-0
info@sieger-design.com
www.sieger-design.com

SPF:architects
8609 Washington Boulevard
Culver City, CA 90232, USA
P. +1 310 558 0902
dafna@spfa.com
www.spfa.com

Stelle Architects
48 Foster Avenue, PO Box 3002
Bridgehampton, NY 11932, USA
P. +1 631 537 0019
info@stelleco.com
www.stelleco.com

Stephen Jolson Architects
58 Greville Street
Prahran 3181, Victoria, Australia
P. +61 3 8656 7100
mail@jolson.com.au
www.jolson.com.au

Tom Ferguson Architecture & Design
Suite 107/59 Marlborough Street
Surry Hills NSW 2010, Australia
P. +61 9698 8850
tom@tfad.com.au
www.tfad.com.au

Yaroslav Rassadin
P. +7 910 445 0143
yaroslav@rassadin.com
www.rassadin.com

Manufacturers:

Alessi USA
155 Spring St, 4th Floor
New York, NY 10012, USA
P: +1 212 431 1310
www.alessi.com

Alno USA
1 Design Center Pl. 634
Boston, MA 02210, USA
Tel. 617-896-2700
www.alno.com

Artificio
www.artificio.es

Arclinea Boston
10 St James Avenue
Boston, MA 02116, USA
P. +1 617 357 9777
info@arclineaboston.com
www.arclineaboston.com

Arwa AG
www.arwa.ch

Balvi
www.balvi.com

Bialetti USA
9409 Buffalo Avenue
Rancho Cucamonga, CA 91730, USA
P. +1 800 421 6290
www.bialetti.com

Big Chill
PO Box 892
Boulder, CO, USA
P. +1 877 842 3269
info@bigchillfridge.com
www.bigchillfridge.com

Binova Spa
www.binova.it

Boffi Spa
www.boffi.com

Bultaup Corporation
P. +1 973 226 5390
www.bultaup.com

Cesar Cucine
www.cesar.it

Conran USA
www.conranusa.com

Dada New York
c/o Modulo 3 Corporation
D/B/A Unifor, 149 Fifth Avenue
New York, NY 10010, USA
P: +1 212 6737106
info@moltenidada.com
www.dadaweb.it

DESU Design
87 Richardson St
Brooklyn, NY 11211, USA
P. +1 718 384 7306
info@desudesign.com
www.desudesign.com

Dica
www.dica.es

Dornbracht Americas Inc.
1700 Executive Drive South, Suite 600
Duluth, GA 30096, USA
P. +1 800 774 1181
mail@dornbracht.com
www.dornbracht.com

Ebanis
www.ebanis.com

Electrolux USA
www.electroluxusa.com

Elica
www.elica.com

Ernesto Meda
www.ernestomeda.it

Fagor America Inc.
Lyndhurst, NJ 07071, USA
P. +1 800 207 0806
info@fagoramerica.com
www.fagoramerica.com

Franke
www.franke.com

Gamadecor
www.gama-decor.com

Habitat
www.habitat.net

Häcker Küchen GmbH & Co KG
www.haecker-kuechen.de

Hardy Inside
www.hardyinside.com

Iitalla
www.iitalla.com

Kohler
444 Highland Drive
Kohler, WI, USA
P. +1 800 456 4537
www.kohler.com

MGS USA
20423 State Rd. 7
F6-291, Boca Raton, FL 33498, USA
P. +1 561 218 8798
info@mgsdesigns.com
www.mgsdesigns.com

Mobalco
www.mobalco.com

Morph UK
Studio 26, 1-3 Berry Street
EC1V oAA, London, UK
P. +44 20 7490 1999
info@morphuk.com
www.morphuk.com

Native Trails
4173 Santa Fe Road, Suite A
San Luis Obispo, CA 93401, USA
P. +1 805 546 8248
mail@nativetrails.net
www.nativetrails.net

Newform
www.newform.it

Normann Copenhagen
www.normann-copenhagen.com

Pando
www.pando.es

Poggenpohl
www.poggenpohl.de

Poliform USA
150 East 58th Street, Floor 6
New York, NY 10155, USA
P. +1 212 421 1220
www.poliformusa.com

Rational
www.rational.de

Rieber GMBH & Co. KG
www.rieber.de

Ritmonio
www.ritmonio.it

Scavolini
www.scavolini.com

Schiffini Mobili Cucine Spa
www.schiffini.it
Sheer
www.sheer.it

SieMatic Ibérica
www.siematic.com

SieMatic Möbelwerke USA
3 Interplex Drive, Suite 101
Feasterville, PA 19053-6960, USA
P. +1 215 604 1350
info@siematic.com
www.siematic.com

Sonoma Stone
www.sonomastone.com

TM Italia
www.tmitalia.com

Vinçon
www.vincon.com